Sustainability of Scheduled Castes:

Taungya Community of Himalayan Region

Sustainability of Scheduled Castes:

Taungya Community of Himalayan Region

Dr Rubina Nusrat

KALPAZ

First Published, 2018

Published by

Kalpaz Publications
C-30, Satyawati Nagar,
Delhi – 110052
E-mail: kalpaz@hotmail.com
Ph.: 9212142040

Printed at: G. Print Process, Delhi

Cataloging in Publication Data—DK
Courtesy: D.K. Agencies (P) Ltd. <docinfo@dkagencies.com>

Nusrat, Rubina, author.
Sustainability of scheduled castes : Taungya community of Himalayan Region / Dr. Rubina Nusrat.
pages cm
Includes bibliographical references.
ISBN 9789386397256

1. Dalits—India—Economic conditions. 2. Dalits—Himalaya Mountains Region—Economic conditions. 3. Community forestry—India. 4. Community forestry—Himalaya Mountains Region. 5. Sustainable development—India. 6. Sustainable development—Himalaya Mountains Region. 7. Rural development—Government policy—India. 8. Rural development—Government policy—Himalaya Mountains Region. I. Title.

LCC HT720.N87 2018 | DDC 305.56880954 23

I want to dedicate this work to
MY DEAREST PARENTS
I miss you both and
GOD bless You.

Contents

Preface

The Book is about the forest dwelling Scheduled Caste Community of Northern Himalayas who are in the process of social exclusion as a result of the afforestation drive conducted at the time of British rule in India. This book discusses the sustainability issues of this tribe in the context of vulnerability and livelihood strategies. The main theme and objective is to make available the literature pertaining to Taungya Community. Since this community is least researched tribe of the region so there is a paucity of secondary literature available on them. Taungya Community are on the verge of cultural extinction due to geographical inaccessibility and are undergoing new pattern of emerging livelihood strategies.

This book elaborates on an overview of the Taungya Community in the context of time and space. It discusses about the sustainability issues of Taungya Community. This book used the sustainable livelihoods framework to describe the livelihood context of Taungya Community: a Scheduled Caste community dwelling in the foothills of Himalayas and drew out implications for Animal Husbandry activities. The sustainable livelihood framework sets out the relationships between the household asset base and factors that exert pressure on the asset base, including policies and institutional processes. It looks at livelihood strategies that are taken to achieve desired outcomes. In the paper, the vulnerability and risks are discussed from the viewpoint of the community itself rather than from an outsiders viewpoint. This framework also emphasises on the interlinkages of the extrinsic factors impacting the livelihood strategies of the respective communities, inferencing on the service delivery and concluding with analysis of opportunities. The asset base vulnerability enhances owing to the external shocks and trends. Animal husbandry plays an important role in sustaining the livelihoods of the resource poor Taungya community in foothills of Himalayas. This book emphasises on the social exclusion of Taungya community.

The chapter emphasises on the levels of women empowerment existing in Taungya community. The factors that lead to maximum and minimum empowerment were devised out and were substantiated with field observations. The women empowerment was further analysed through the usage of Naila Kabeers' concept of the Social Relations Approach to conduct a gender analysis of the women empowerment in Taungya community of Uttarakhand and Uttar Pradesh. Gender analysis framework and the tools provided in it elucidate a pre-designed methodology for researching the linkages between concepts given in Social Relations approach of the development in human well being, Social relations and institutional analysis. This analysis aimed at exploring how the livelihood activities and institutions lead to transformations in the gender roles and norms, henceforth, consequently to factors effecting empowerment of Taungya women. This content has been published in a journal *South Asian Journal of Participative Development*.

Besides the book provides book references to the detailed coverage of all specific concepts and frameworks and is perhaps the quickest way of all to gain access to the knowledge regarding Taungya community and their sustainability aspect.

This book has a readership of academicians and researchers who are working on sustainability and marginalised communities, displacement and resettlement of Tribals, Livelihood strategies and women empowerment in Tribal communities.

Acknowledgements

My most thankfulness goes to the Almighty God for His great assistance to me all over the years in all my endeavours.

My deepest thanks goes to the respondents of this study who opened their hearts and homes to me like a family member and provided me with an opportunity of getting an insight into their day-to-day life without which this partially ethnographic work was next to impossible.

This memorable occasion provides me a unique opportunity to express my profound sense of gratitude and reverence to Professor B.K. Pattanaik for his constant inspiration. I consider myself extremely fortunate for the opportunity to work under the scholastic and esteem guidance of Dr N.A. Farooquee whose perpetual encouragements helped in extending my research curiosity. Without his deep interest in my research, I would definitely not be able to complete this daunting task in a prompt and efficient manner. Special thanks and gratitude also go to Dr Nisha Varghese for giving me her advice and her contribution is untold in my life. I must mention that my friend Mr Nabikant Jha whose persistent questioning led to venturing into unexplored answers.

I am also grateful to *Pradhan* of Tongia Villages Ms Renu and Forest officer Mr Shukla for their continuous cordial support and friendship throughout the field work in Uttar Pradesh and Uttarakhand. My special thanks also go to Forest guard Mr Wasir and NGO worker Mr Nazim for their great assistance during my field work.

I remain indebted to my father Mr Nusrat Husain who has been my life support, holding my hand with innate strength while allowing me to explore new heights. I would like to express deepest gratitude to my beloved mother, brothers, sisters and mother-in-law for their understanding, patience, inspiration, sacrifices and blessings without which this study would not possible.

Last but not the least; I thank my husband Mr Syed Yousuf Qaseem-had it not been for him, this research would not have seen the end of the road. It was he who consistently encouraged me to continue despite all adversities that I faced due to difficult field area. I thank him whole heartedly for all his support and effortlessly taking care of our son S. Ibrahim Yousuf by compensating for my persistent long absence during my field visits.

Of course, I have mentioned only the prominent few who have contributed to the work. But many more remain unmentioned inadvertently. It is their help and co-operation which has enabled me to complete this work.

Rubina Nusrat

List of Tables

List of Figures

Chapter - 1

Evolution of Taungya

Evolution of Taungya System: An Overview

Taungya is a land use management system which consists of the raising of forest crops in conjunction with temporary agricultural crops in which a short phase of food crop production is used as a silvicultural method to ensure the establishment of timber trees (King, 1968; Evans, 1982; Wiersum, 1982). Taungya is a type of agroforestry. Agroforestry is a symbiosis of tree growing, crop production and livestock raising where each component is beneficial to each other.

Taungya is a Burmese word, but it is believed that the system is much older, having originated in China. The word is reported to have originated, in Myanmar (Burma) and means hill (*Taung*) cultivation (*ya*) (Blanford, 1958). Originally it was the local term for shifting cultivation, and was subsequently used to describe the afforestation method.

Taungya is a Burmese word meaning shifting cultivation in hills. Farmer are temporarily allotted government land and contracted to plant specific tree species. While the trees are young and before the canopy closes, the farmers are allowed to plant food and cash crops for their own benefit while maintaining the tree. It is the first step towards the agroforestry. After a few years when the trees begin to shade the land the farmers move to another part of the land and the whole operation is repeated.

Taungya community are the settled villages on the peripheries of forests in Uttar Pradesh and Uttarakhand. These are labour families who migrated from West Bengal at the time of Britishers for afforestation drive by the Forest Department of Uttar Pradesh. They were settled in villages by the Forest Department with an allotment of one acre of land per family, a well for drinking water and a primary school for the children. Taungya system was banned in 1985 in the forests of Uttar Pradesh. Taungya or Taungyas is used in this study interchangeably.

Types of Taungya

Taungya system is known by different names, some of which are also used to denote shifting cultivation: Tumpangsari in Indonesia; Kaingining in the Philippines; *Ladang* in Malaysia; *Chena* in Sri Lanka; *Kumri, Jhooming, Ponam, Taila,* and *Tuckle* in different parts of India; *Shamba* in East Africa; *Parcelero* in Puerto Rico; *Consorciarcao* in Brazil, etc. (King, 1968). Most of the forest plantations that have been established in the tropical world, particularly in Asia and Africa, owe their origin to the Taungya system (von Hesmer, 1966, 1970; King, 1979).

In India, three types of Taungya systems are in practice:

Departmental Taungyas

In this system, labourers are employed to cultivate food crops in the interspace of tree lines to suppress weeds. This system is followed especially in irrigated plantations.

Leased Taungyas

The interspaces among the tree lines is leased to public for cultivation of crops for a period of two or three years after felling operations. Following this method the entire cost of forest regeneration is met from the leased money.

Village Taungyas

The available area of cleared forest is divided among the villagers settled in the forest. Usually a family gets about 0.2 to 0.4 ha of land for three to five years. Many times entire work of tending, felling and regeneration including seed collection is done by the Taungya villagers and they are allowed to cultivate agricultural crops in the interspaces or sometimes one to two years before plantations starts.

A large number of agricultural crops are grown in the interspaces depending on the requirement of the villagers including spice crops like cinnamon, nutmeg, pepper, coffee and medicinal plants.

Several alternatives and improvements to Taungya systems have been initiated in different places, most of them with the objective of providing better living and social conditions for the participating farmers. One of the most widely quoted examples is the Forest Village Scheme in Thailand, which has generated several reports and also the Modified Taungya System in Ghana (Agyeman *et al.,* 2003).

Taungya: Global Perspectives

Taungya is a land use system in which peasants are allowed to cultivate agricultural crops for the first few years between the planted seedlings of forest plantations. Taungya is a land management system which consists of the raising of forest crops in conjunction with temporary agricultural crops in which a short phase of food crop production is used as a silvicultural method to ensure the establishment of timber species (King, 1968; Evans, 1982; Wiersum, 1982).

Taungya system was promoted in Burma in 1855 by Sir Dietrich Brandis to arrest the destructive effects of shifting cultivation (von Hesmer, 1966), and Annual reports on forest administration in Burma showed that teak plantations began in 1863 in Burma (MacGillivray, 1990). Today the Taungya system is known by different names, some of which are also used to denote shifting cultivation. Blanford (1958) reported that the word Taungya originated and practiced in Myanmar (Burma) and means hill (Taung) and cultivation (ya). Taunyga system is therefore, essentially a modification of the traditional shifting cultivation, but various forms can be found in different parts of the tropics (Nair, 1984). Gorman (1969) mentioned that evidence from excavations at Ban Chieng, North-eastern Thailand, indicated that people have cultivated plants in the area for centuries. The system involved combinations of trees, root crops and seed crops. In Africa, it was reported to have been first introduced in Kenya as early as in 1920's. Taungya system has been employed to establish plantations successfully at low establishment costs in South East Asia, East Africa, and West Africa including Ghana. Taungya system is considered to be one of the low-cost forms of government compensatory forest plantation establishment which enlists farmers who are willing to plant and care for forest crops in return for being allowed to grow food crops for four to five years while the trees are young (Enabor, 1975; Goswani, 1982; Watson, 1983). Biologically and economically, the Taungya system has proven to be a successful partial integration of food crops and tree husbandry. In the America (Weaver, 1989), it is practised most extensively in South-east Asia. As such, recent improvements in Taungya plantations have occurred principally in South Asia.

The Development of Taungya System in Burma

According to King (1968), the origin of Taungya system can be traced back to the 1850s in Burma, where the system was used as a means of replanting teak on badly degraded land. In 1806, U. Pan Hle, a Karen in the Tonze forests of Thararrawaddy Division in Myanmar (Burma), established a plantation of *Tectona grandis* by using the Taungya system that the Governor, Sir Dietrich Brandis considered the method of the Taungya system as the most efficient way of planting teak (Blanford, 1958), and reported that U Pan Hle, a Karen tribesman, might have first used the Taungya system for the establishment of teak plantations as early as 1856. Taungya was introduced in Thailand in 1911, Malaysia in 1950 and Indonesia in 1873 (Awang, 1985). According to Hailey (1957), Taungya system became widespread and was introduced into South Africa as early as 1887. Again, in 1890, Taungya system was taken from Burma to the Chittagong and Bengal areas in colonial India (Raghavan, 1960). Most of the forest plantations established in the tropical world, particularly in Asia and Africa, owe their origin to the Taungya system (von Hesmer, 1966; King, 1979). The Forest Department restricted popular forest access but also promoted new patterns of co-operation. The most concerted attempt to win the support of forest users concerned the hill Karen. Control of the teak forests required the restriction of Taungya practices but also convinced Brandis that shifting cultivation could be turned to advantage. In 1856, Brandis had encouraged cultivators to sow teak with their rice and cotton crops after noting the beneficial effect of Taungyas on young teak in the Prome district. After the experiment succeeded, the department sought to introduce Taungya forestry on a systematic basis. The hill Karen, however, refused to alter their lifestyle and this stance was the source of their initial refusal to participate in the reforestation scheme. Lieutenant William Seaton approached Karen in Tharrawaddy district in 1863, finding them strongly opposed to a system that would gradually undermine their independent lifestyle by converting cultivable areas into reserved forests from which they would be excluded. [Karen headmen] openly admit that they look upon the sowing of teak in their 'yas' [Taungyas] as taking the bread from the child's mouth. All that they urge to prove this is true enough. Every one is aware of the fact of their returning to the same localities to Cut yas after a lapse of from 10 to 15 years. To overcome such opposition, forest officials alternatively enticed and compelled Karen compliance. In lieu of a fine for violating forest rules, officials often required cultivators to plant teak in the clearings. At the same time, forest officials rewarded voluntary participation. Benefits included tax exemption, direct payments for planting, and provision of designated lands for the Karen's own use. In 1868-69, a Karen village in the Mokka-Beeling reserve (Tharrawaddy division) agreed to plant teak in their Taungyas and more soon followed, attracted primarily by the promise of land.

Table 1.1: A Typical Programme of Work to be carried out in the Taungya System in 1920 in Burma

The year before regeneration	
December	Allotment of areas to Taungya participants to be completed.
January	Cutting to commerce.
March	Cutting to be completed.
First year of regeneration	
March and April	Collection of seed to be completed.
April	Burning to be completed not later than 20th April.
May	Heaping and reburning of unburnt refuse to be completed.
May	Staking and sowing of tree seeds at stake and broad casting of accessory species to be completed. In the case of teak, sowing should if possible be completed on suitable plots throughout the area by 30th April.
May to June	Sowing of field crops.
July	Inspection of lines and stakes and planting up of blanks.

(*contd...*)

July to November	Tending of tree seedlings in conjunction with the field crops.
November and December	Reaping of field crops.
January	Clearing of lines, restaking and counting of seedlings surviving and payment of Taungya participants. Survey to be carried out and inspection paths made.
March	Fire protection.
The second year	
April and May	Fire protection to be continued up to the break of the rains.
May	First weeding and filling of gaps to be completed by the end of May or 15th June at latest.
September	Second weeding.
March	Fire protection.
The third year	
April and May	Fire protection until the break of the rains.
June	First weeding.
September	Second weeding if necessary.
March	Fire protection.
The fourth year	
April and May	Fire protection until the break of the rains.
June and July	Cleaning if necessary.
March	Fire protection.
The fifth year	
April and May	Fire protection.
November and December	Cleaning creeper cutting and thinning After Blanford, 1925.

Note: the year should be taken as the forest year, i.e.
1st April to 31st March.

The Development of Taungya System in Ghana

In Ghana, Taungya system was introduced as far back as in 1928 when the then Forestry Department was charged with the responsibility of establishing forest plantations for the production of wood in the long term and also to meet the needs of farmers for fertile land in areas where farm land outside the national permanent forest estate was infertile and limited (Brookman-Amissah, 1978). This was in the right direction, because in most tropical countries, people living in forest fringe communities are usually part of the poorest and least powerful of the stakeholders. They are socially and economically marginalised and face escalation of socio-economic stress due to lack of education, legal or political support. So, interested farmers were, however, given new land to continue the Taungya system. According to Forestry Department (1991), Taungya practice started as early as 1929 in the Brimso forest reserve with *Senna siamea* as the major tree species. Taungya plantation establishment intensified in Ghana between 1969 and 1985 (FD, 1985) as part of the 'Operation Feed Yourself' Programme. Despite the supposed advantages of the Taungya system, it has not been widely adopted and has virtually come to a halt. The tendency of Taungya farmers to pay more attention to their agricultural crops and to neglect the tree crops made the system unreliable in the past that resulted in its discontinuation in 1985.

Irrespective of the problems with the failed traditional Taungya system, forest fringe communities still viewed the Taungya system as one of the most beneficial forest tenure systems and requested the Ghana Government to re-introduce it albeit with changes to make it more efficient. The Ghana Government has, therefore, reintroduced the Taungya with modifications termed as Modified Taungya System (MTS).

The Modified Taungya System

Under the Modified Taungya System (MTS), being operated in Ghana, Taungya farmers are now fully involved in the establishment and maintenance of the plantations. The farmers tend food and tree crops that are planted in a mixture on the same plot until such a time that the canopy closure of the growing trees makes it impractical to continue with crop cultivation. After canopy closure, the Taungya farmers continue to tend the trees until maturity. Farmers are, therefore, eligible for a share of the benefits accruing from the plantation according to the benefit-sharing framework, which ensure greater benefit flows to participating farmers (Agyeman *et al.,* 2003).

The Development of Taungya System in Kenya: The Shamba System

The Shamba system is a highly developed form of Taungya system practiced on State forest land in Kenya where there is considerable integration of the cultivators into the Forest Department (Nair, 1984).

According to Evans (1982), Shamba system features were adapted later in Nigeria and Trinidad respectively. The Shamba system when properly practiced could allow sustained, optimum production of food crops along with forestry species from the same piece of land and thus, meet most of the social and economic needs of the farmers. The economic implications of Shamba system are derived from the sale of agricultural products. The system also provides more or less full-time employment to most Shamba farmers who have no other sources of income. For the Forestry Department, Shamba system is a cost-effective method of tree establishment. Apart from providing a weed-free area for tree planting, it also ensures weeding around young trees for two to three years so that tree survival rates increase. In addition to the weeding benefits, fire control is also an important reason for inter-planting agricultural crops with tree crops in Taungya system (White, 1985). Other social benefits provided by the Forestry Department in the specifics of the Shamba system agreement included free housing, medical facilities, schools, welfare and infrastructural development (Wanyeki, 1981). The Shamba system seems to be the most appropriate land-use-system for rural development and poverty alleviation programmes. The combination of agriculture and forestry when properly implemented reduces environmental degradation and also provides means of reconciling the often-conflicting interest of tropical foresters and farmers. The system also satisfies most social and economic needs of subsistence farmers who participate in it, and save the forest from the destruction caused by shifting cultivation (White, 1985). Irrespective of the enormous benefits associated with Shamba system, it is also characterised by a number of drawbacks.

Wanyeki (1981) found out that;

(a) about 40 per cent of the reported forest fires in Kenya originated as a result of Shamba practice, mostly at the time of clearing;

(b) the possible damage to crops by wild animals such as elephants, buffaloes discourages some participants, particularly in remote areas;

(c) the cultivation of grasslands in the forest areas has reduced grazing land for both livestock and wild animals;

(d) it requires high levels of supervision, otherwise the laid-down regulations would not be followed, thereby affecting tree growth adversely;

(e) in some areas the number of participants far exceeds the available land, thus leading to illegal clearing.

The Development of Taungya System in Thailand: Forest Village System

Forest Village System is practiced in Thailand and combines the advantage of reforestation and subsistence agriculture. The original Burmese colonial Taungya system considered improvement in social forestry in which there is intensive use of labour. This employment increases income and community stability (Segustron, 1976; Gregersen, 1982). There are many opportunities for workers to earn wages in the Forest Village system and since majority of the rural people have few assets other than their capacity to work, they seem to benefit from the Forest Village System.

The Development of Taungya System in Indonesia: Tumpangsari

This is a system of Taungya employed by the Forestry Estate Enterprise in Indonesia for reforestation, especially teak (Siregar, 1990) in areas with a pronounced dry season, and the expectation is for an 80-years rotation.

In Tumpangsari, a contract is made between individual farmers and the Forestry Estate Enterprise. The contract specifies the area to be planted, the period of agricultural cultivation, and the kind of crops to be planted as well as the amount of money to be paid for tree planting and tending. In this system, each family is allotted 0.25-hectare plot to be inter-cropped with the planted tree seedlings for two years, and the agricultural crops include dry land rice, maize, pepper, peanuts soybeans. Under certain conditions, cassava also is permitted. On sloping land, erosion control structures are built with stones or dead trees and branches. Other control measures include drainage ditches, and planting along contours (Wiersum, 1982).

Intensified Taungya Cultivation

Increasing use of high-yielding agricultural crop varieties and modern cropping practices were incorporated in the Taungya system in Indonesian agricultural enterprise in the 1960. In 1972, the Indonesian State Forest Enterprise tested the feasibility of such agricultural improvement for the Taungya system that proved successful with dry land rice production by increasing yield of rice from 700 kg to 3740 kg per hectare (Wiersum, 1981). According to Wiersum (1981), the system was developed further, based on research carried out by the Forest Faculty of the Gadjah Mada University. Kartasubrata (1997) and Wiersum (1982) mentioned that the system for intensive Taungya system was developed with the following characteristic features:

(a) utilisation of selected high-yielding varieties of the main food crops;
(b) better practices for land preparation and soil tillage;
(c) minimum use of fertilisers;
(d) control of pest and diseases;
(e) correct timing of planting and fertilising with respect to the rainfall.

According to Sumitro (1990), the Forest Service encouraged the Taungya farmers to embark on the intensive Taungya system on a wider scale in almost all the districts in Indonesia with the following objectives:

(a) to contribute to the national food production;
(b) to provide more employment opportunities to under-employment farmers;
(c) to increase the income and welfare of the forest fringe communities;
(d) to safeguard forest plantations;
(e) to maximise returns of the land which is the most scarce production factor in the forest fringe communities.

The Development of Taungya System in China

There are many variations of Taungya in China, but they fall into three general patterns with each pattern predominating in a different region. Huo (1992) has emphasised on three major patterns of Taungya in China which are given below:

Pattern I: Trees+ Crops in the North China Plain

Since the palin is the country's most important farming area owing to it being a juncture of Yellow, Huai and Hai Rivers. However, for Taungya agriculture, commercially valuable timber species such as Poplar, Willow, Elm, Chinese scholartree, Black locust, Toon (Ailanthus altissima), Paulownia and Catalpas are planted. The trees themselves are important for harvest in Chinese Taungya. They must grow fast and be of good timber quality. Paulownia is frequently favoured by farmers because of its rooting habit.This rooting habit makes Paulownia a good tree with which to intercrop agricultural crops and there appears to be little competition between Paulownia and crops for nutrients and water. Paulownia is also desirable because the species has an open crown through which a large proportion of incoming light can penetrate. Paulownia in China forms its leaves relatively late, in late April to early May, and thus summer-harvested crops can get a good start. Paulownia looses its leaves in mid-November and its mulch seems to help prevent frost damage to autumn crops.

In Taungya, where crops are interplanted between the Paulownia, the trees should be planted in rows 20-30 m apart, and with 3-6 m intervals within the rows. This spacing gives the desirable microclimate when the trees are young. After 5-6 years, alternate rows of trees are harvested, leaving the final rows 40-60 m apart. Pruning of lower branches of Paulownia improves crop yield, apparently because this practice increases the light reaching the crop. Many medicinal herbs and some kinds of vegetables such as celery, ginger and day lily are partially shade tolerant and have higher yield in partial shade. These species may be planted closer to the Paulowmia, or in plantations where Paulownia is spaced more closely. Interplanting agricultural crops between rows of Paulownia increased yields on summer harvested crops as well as some autumn harvested crops.

Pattern II. Taxiium + Crop+ Fishery in Wetlands of Huai Plain and the Middle–Lower Yangtze Plain

Most wetlands in this region of China are already terraced, but adaptation to moist conditions is still a factor in selecting trees for agroforestry. Pond cypress performs best in agroforestry systems.The species is fast growing and its stem is straight and has good wood quality. It sheds its needles in late October and renews its foliage in April. Thus, underplanted winter crops have the benefit of full sunlight. Other preferable gymnosperms are swamp cypress and water fir. The long-peduncled alder is one of the most preferred deciduous hardwoods. These four species are the most popular for wetland Taungya agroforestry in this region of China.

In these wetland systems, Wheat, Barley, Oat, Oilseed rape and Broad bean are commonly planted in late autumn and are harvested at the end of the next spring. For deeper ponds, water lily, water lettuce and water caltrop are cultivated as floating crops.There are approximately 40 kinds of fish utilised in fish breeding, including common carp, black and golden carp and bighead.

Pattern III. Chinese Fir+ Crops, or Chinese Fir+ Tugoil Trees+ Crops in Mountainous areas of the subtropics of China

There are variety of crops in the subtropics of China which are used in Taungya agroforestry.

1. *Food crops:* Wheat, Buckwheat, Millet, dryland Rice, Taro, Cowpea, Sweet potato and Cassava.
2. *Oil-bearing crops:* Soybean, Peanut, Oilseed rape, Sesame, Tungoil tree and Cubeb litsea tree.
3. *Economic crops:* Tobacco, Cotton, Ginger, Chinese indigo, Ramie and Pineapple.
4. *Medicinal herbs:* Dandshen, Large headed atractylodes, Purple flowered peucedanum, Chinese gromwell, Safflower and Job's tears.

Types of Taungya in China

Chinese fir is usually planted with a spacing of 2 × 2.5 m or 3 m. Two general types of Taungya are used:

1. Chinese fir + crops

One year old Chinese fir trees are interplanted with high stalk crops such as corn. The corn overtops the fir. The second year, millet is interplanted between the fir and the height of the millet and fir is approximately the same. The third year, soyabeans are interplanted and they form a low cover beneath the crowns of the fir.

2. Chinese fir + Tungoil tree or cubeb tree + crops

This system works better on more fertile soils. The seeds of the Tungoil tree are sown at the same time that the Chinese fir seedlings or cuttings are planted for every tungoil tree.

History of Taungya in India

When the British invaded India 250 years ago, they found the sub-continent covered with a mosaic of vegetation they did not comprehend. Tall dark trees, gnarled and knotted creepers, wild grasslands- the sheer tropical abundance of India's forests shocked, overwhelmed them. Ultimately, forests came to signify a number of simpler issues (or things): snakes, tigers, barbarians/rebels, pests, and adventure. British colonisers/traders never neglected the mundane and practical, though, which lay beyond this 'exotic' and 'orient'. The East India Company went on 'empire-building' and the first 100 years of British rule witnessed a colossal plunder of half of India's forest vegetation. Resultant timbers went to feed the railways and the new and old shipyards in both India and England. The 'cleared' land were settled to white planters (tea, coffee, indigo and sugarcane), and the native 'zamindars', the new class of feudal lords that the British created.

The carnage would not stop before 1860, when a century of empire-building and associated political stresses and compulsions would make the rulers wiser, and in many areas—for instance, areas under administrative control of 'native' Kings and Nawabs—forests would be let alone. A different fate awaited forests within the empire. In 1864, the first forest administration for the British Empire (Imperial Forest Service) was created. In 1868 and 1878, India was 'endowed' with its first forest policy and forest act, which, prescribed, among other things, banishing indigenous communities from the forest and restricting forest usage by them. In the interests of the queen and empire, the British proclaimed all 'unsettled' and 'ownerless' common property resources like pastures and forests 'eminent domain', which meant that the colonial state would 'manage' the forests as it saw fit. 'Management' of resources (the British called it scientific forest management) was the key, which, the Indian forest policy claimed would make forests more homogenous and productive. Accordingly, in between 1864 and 1947 (when the British left India), Indian forests were taught 'order', with neat rows of tall and elegant pines filling up the hillsides, and *sal* (Shorea robusta) and *teak* (Tectona grandis) monocultures replacing the riffraff (in vernacular Hindi *'jhar'*). In fact, forests were increasingly being managed as estates and forest villages (new colonies of plantation workers) were being set up inside forests. Later, when Dietrich Brandis, the 'father of Indian forestry', developed the 'Taungya' system of plantation, many of these villages came to be known as 'Taungyas'. Taungya became the premiere plantation method not only in India, but also several Asian and African countries.

In 1856, when Dietrich Brandis was in Burma, then part of British India, shifting cultivation was widespread and there were several court cases against the villagers for encroaching on the forest reserves. Brandis realised the detrimental effect of shifting cultivation on the management of timber resources and encouraged the practice of "regeneration of teak (*Tectona grandis*) with the assistance of Taungya," (Blanford, 1958) based on the well known German system of *Waldfeldbau*, which involved the cultivation of agricultural crops in forests. Two decades later the system proved so efficient that teak plantations were established at a very low cost. The villagers, who were given the right to cultivate food crops in the early stages of plantation establishment, no longer had to defend themselves in court cases on charges of forest destruction; they promoted afforestation on the cleared land by sowing teak seeds. The Taungya system was soon introduced into other parts of British India, and later it spread throughout Asia, Africa, and Latin America.

Taungya system was introduced in India by Brandis in 1856.The first Taungya plantations were raised in 1863 in North Bengal, in 1886 in Sylhet and in 1890 in Coorg. However, regular Taungya cultivation was not taken up until 1911 when it was used for raising Shorea robusta plantation in North Bengal, where it was soon extended to Tectona

Grandis in 1912. It was not until 1923 that it was adopted to regenerate failed *Sal* (Shorea Robusta) coppice coups in UP. In South India, the system is referred to as Kumri cultivation.

Table 1.2: Major Agroforestry Practices followed in India

Practice	*Agroecological Region / States*
(Listed in alphabetical order)	
Boundary planting and live hedges	In all regions throughout the country.
Farm woodlots	
Homegardens	Mainly tropical west coast region, especially Kerala, southern Karnataka, Andaman and Nicobar Islands.
Industrial plantations with crops	Intensively cropped areas in northern and northwestern regions: Haryana, Himachal Pradesh, Punjab, Uttar Pradesh; also in southern states (Andhra Pradesh, Karnataka, Kerala, and Tamil Nadu).
Scattered trees on farms, parklands	All regions, especially semiarid and arid regions.
Shaded perennial systems with plantation crops	Mainly humid tropical region in the southern region; also Assam, W. Bengal.
Shelterbelts and windbreaks	In wind-prone areas, esp. coastal, arid, and alpine regions.
Silvopasture: Fodder trees	throughout the country.
Intercropping/grasses with fruit trees Seasonal forest grazing	
Subtropical and tropical; orchards in hilly regions	Semiarid and mountainous eco-system.
Taungya	Eastern region.
Tree planting for reclamation of saline soils and wastelands	Semiarid and canal-irrigated regions, mostly in the northern and north-western regions.
Woodlots for soil conservation	In hilly areas, along sea coast and ravine lands.

Source: S. Puri and P.K.R. Nair, 2004.

Ecologically, Taungya brought the much-needed fire component back both to tropical and temperate forest systems. Socio-politically, it offered a temporary solution to the problem of increasing tribal unrest in forest areas of British India. Taungya villages had some sort of 'rehabilitation' space for displaced '*jhumiyas*' (shifting cultivators), where they could clearfell forests and burn the area to raise food-crops.

The cultivators then had to raise plantations in that land. During initial years of Taungya, this labour was mandatory '*beggar*'-the cultivators received no wages. Despite this, Taungyas showed some improvements on pre-Taungya forest villages. In Bengal, for instance, 'permanent' forest villages started to come up from 1910 onwards, where settlers signed agreement papers or bonds with the Department. These agreements spelt out some privileges for forest villagers, like free timber and other implements for building quarters, firewood and fodder—in addition to cultivable land.

Taungya, according to Tejwani (1987) begun in India in the nineteenth century as a means to exploit the cheap labour of landless peasants in establishing plantations of economically valuable trees, especially Sal (*Shorea robusta*) and Teak (*Tectona grandis*), and today, Taungya is practiced in several region of India whereby different kinds of agricultural crops are integrated with the tree crops (Table 1.3).

Table 1.3: Spread of Taungya and Crops integrated in India

State	Tree crops	Associated agricultural crops
Uttar Pradesh	*Shorea robusta* *Tectona grandis* *Acacia catechu* *Dalbergia sisoo* *Eucalyptus spp.* *Populus spp.*	Maize, paddy, sorghum pigeon pea, soybean wheat, barley, chickpea, oilseed rape.
Andhra Pradesh	*Anacardium occidentale* *Tectona grandis*	Hill paddy, groundnut, sweet potato
	Bombax ceiba *Eucalyptus spp.*	Bamboo
Kerala	*Tectona grandis* *Bombax ceiba* *Eucalyptus spp.*	Paddy, Manihot spp., ginger, tumeric
Assam	*Shorea robusta*	Paddy
Tamil Nadu	*Tectona grandis* *Santalum album* *Tamarindus indica* *Acacia nilotica* *Acacia mearnsil* *Ceiba pentandra*	Millets, pulses, groundnut, potato, cotton, Manihot, Cashew, Rubber, Bamboo

(contd...)

West Bengal	*Tectona grandis* *Shorea robusta* *Schima wallichii* *Cryptomeria japonica* *Quercus spp.* *Michelia doltsopa*	Paddy, Maize, millets, turmeric, ginger, ladies finger, pineapple, hemp
Maharastra	*Shorea robusta*	Sunhemp, jute, mesta, sunflower, castor
Andaman	*Pterocarpus dalbergoides*	Sugarcane, maize

Source: Tejwani (1987).

Taungya in Uttar Pradesh

By the early 1930s, the Forest Department in Uttar Pradesh recognised that its existing system of growing and managing forest plantations was unsuccessful, and was looking for alternatives. Labours were invited to the area in the early 1930s under the sponsorship of the Forest Department. The arrangement involved the labours planting and maintaining plantations, and growing crops for themselves for the first few years in between the rows. As the plantations grew up, they would move their crops and start a new plantation. In addition, they were given a small amount of land for traditional agricultural purposes (one acre per family), and rights to grazing and the extraction of fuelwood and *bhabbar* grass from the forest. This system of plantation was called Taungya system and labours involved as Taungya people.The aim of Taungya move was to regenerate forest cover and exploit it for commercial gains. The Forest Department, however, viewed them as a transitory work force, they did not have the right to *pucca* houses and their villages were not accorded revenue status, thus barring them from access to development funds, local voting rights and a gram sabha.

The Taungyas were no longer needed by the Forest Department after the end of commercial forestry operations in the area and the initiation of the proposed park in the 1980s. The Forest Department denied that they had any permanent settlement rights, and demanded that the four villages within the proposed park boundary were vacated.The FD used Taungyas till 1980s when it was decided to do away with the practice but community was not given the land promised as remuneration. Instead, the community was declared encroachers and barred from using forest produce even for domestic purpose.

That's when, in 50 years from 1930 to 1980 Taungya dedicated themselves to forestation, which includes 10,000 hectare in Shivalik area, covering Saharanpur and Haridwar, 20,000 hectare (Kusmi jungle) in Gorakhpur,10,000 hectare in Dehradun division and 15,000 hectare in Kheri (Kothari, 2011).

Fig. 1.1: Taungya plantation.

Today, there are over 100 Taungya vangrams with a population of around two lakh in UP. They work as daily wagers and have no access to basic facilities such as education and health. Their names are in electoral rolls but do not exist in revenue records, hence they cannot get below poverty line cards or domicile certificates and don't qualify as guarantors for bank loans and bail in legal cases Taungya plantations in Uttar Pradesh are found in Saharanpur, Bijnor, Lakhimpur Kheri, Pilibhit, Gorakhpur, Shravasti, Balrampur, Bahraich, Basti and Gonda among other places. Till the community worked for FD, it got some facilities like primary schools but these were withdrawn after being declared encroachers. The schools were demolished and Taungyas were barred from venturing into forest land.

Latest Developments in Uttar Pradesh

Living a legally non-existent life for more than six decades, the Taungya forest-dwellers in Gorakhpur and Maharajganj districts of Uttar Pradesh finally got their share of rights on forestland.

On July 25, State Forest Minister Fateh Bahadur Singh distributed land titles to 651 Taungya families in six villages of the two districts under Forest Rights Act (FRA), 2006 (Kumar, 2011).

Taungyas were hired by the Forest Department as bonded labourers to plant trees in degraded forests of Uttar Pradesh during the British rule. But later, they were branded illegal forest-settlers. Neither the Forest Department nor the revenue department recognised them.

But the FRA promises the rights of forest-dwellers on the forestland and resources they traditionally use. In 2009, more than 4,500 Taungya families of Gorakhpur and Maharajganj filed claims for ownership of the land they were living on. After much reluctance, the government finally started accepting these claims. On July 25, 147 titles were distributed in Bharivaisee village of Maharajganj, while 504 titles were distributed in five forest villages of Gorakhpur district—Tilkunia (212), Rajeji Camp (85), Rajehi Khale (47), Aambagh (101) and Chillwa (59). The applications of 17 Taungya villages in Maharajganj are being processed and land titles may soon be distributed. Applications for community rights over the forestland are also being considered. Living a legally non-existent life for more than six decades, the Taungya forest-dwellers in Gorakhpur and Maharajganj districts of Uttar Pradesh finally got their share of rights on forestland. On July 25, state forest minister Fateh Bahadur Singh distributed land titles to 651 Taungya families in six villages of the two districts under Forest Rights Act (FRA), 2006. (Kumar Sambhav S., 2011).

Chapter - 2

Sustainability and Rural Welfare Schemes

India is an agrarian and developing country with 6,38,365 villages. Nearly 74.00 per cent of the people live in villages. According to the agricultural census report (1990-91), 105.29 million operational holdings in the country were classified as small farms and marginal farms. There were over 74.6 million agricultural labourers/workers in the country representing about 25.00 per cent of the total labourers. With such a large number of small holdings as well as agricultural labourers as farm servants, the incidence of unemployment, under-employment and disguised-unemployment is very large. Most of agricultural labourers could get employment for less than 180 days per annum, and the employment is only for few hours and it is at a level much below their productive and earning capacity. The rate of growth of employment has declined sharply from 2.04 per cent per year during the period 1983-94 to only 0.98 per cent per year during the period 1994 - 2000. There was sharp decelaration in the growth of labour force from 2.05 per cent during the period 1983-94 to only 1.03 per cent during the period 1994-2000. Overall employment growth accelerated to 2.8 per cent during 1999-2005. But the average daily status unemployment rate, which had increased from 6.1 per cent in 1993-94 to 7.3 per cent in 1999-00, increased further to 8.3 per cent in 2004-05. Currently, this rate is around 9 per cent (61st NSSO survey). It indicates that many people are not getting regular employment. It is clear that India has not been able to meet the employment demand.

The creation of employment opportunities with food security has been an important objective of developmental planning in India. The relatively higher growth of population and labour force has led to an increase in the volume of unemployment and underemployment from one plan period to another. The Government of India aim to bring employment through wage and self-employment into a larger focus with the goal of reducing unemployment and underemployment to a negligible level and of providing food security against hunger. Such an approach is necessary because it is realised that larger and efficient use of available human and other resources is the most effective way of alleviating poverty, reducing inequalities, improving nutritional levels and sustaining a reasonably high pace of economic growth.

The government has initiated several employment programmes, which have been detailed below:

Wage Employment Programmes

Wage employment programmes formed an important component of the anti-poverty strategy. They not only provide employment opportunities during lean agricultural seasons but also in times of floods, droughts and other natural calamities. They create rural infrastructure which supports further economic activity. These programmes also put an upward pressure on market wage rates by attracting people to public works programmes, thereby reducing labour supply and pushing up demand for labour. Major thrust to wage employment programmes in the country was provided only after the attainment of self-sufficiency in food grains in the 1970's. The National Rural Employment Programme (NREP) and Rural Landless Employment Guarantee Programmes (RLEGP) were started in the sixth and seventh five year plans.

National Rural Employment Programme (NREP)

The NREP was launched in 1980 as a centrally sponsored scheme on 50:50 sharing basis between the centre and the states. The three main objectives of the scheme were:

- Generating additional gainful employment
- Creating durable community assets
- Improving overall quality of life in rural areas

All type of work which aim at creating durable community assets as village road, ponds, water bodies etc., were undertaken in the programme. The identified works based on the felt needs of the rural community are passed in the Gram Sabha. Later on these projects are implemented through the village panchayats.

Rural Landless Employment Guarantee Programme (RLEGP)

RLEGP was launched in the year 1983. The main goal of the programme was to generate additional employment in rural areas particularly for the landless workers. The programme was a central scheme, fully funded by the Central Government. The programme like the NREP also aimed at improving the quality of life of the people living in rural areas and to create productive and durable assets for strengthening rural infrastructure.

Food for Work Programme (FFWP)

FFWP was launched in the year 1977. The aim was to generate additional gainful employment in rural areas, create durable community assets, strength social and rural infrastructure and to raise standard of living. The wages were paid in the form of foodgrains and government surplus stocks were used for the purpose of ensuring food grain supply. Some of the important objectives of the programme are:

- To provide supplementary resources along with other aids to the rural poor of the backward districts.
- To provide supplementary wage employment to the poor rural populace of the backward districts.
- To provide security pertaining to food to the rural poor of the backward districts.
- To facilitate the creation of common economic and social assets for the rural areas.

Jawahar Rozgar Yojana/Jawahar Gram Samridhi Yojana

JRY was launched in 1989 by merging the two schemes such as NREP and RLEGP. The JRY aims to alleviate poverty through creating supplementary employment opportunities for the rural poor during agricultural slack periods. The other objectives of the scheme are creation of social assets such as roads, public forests, school building etc. The fund under JRY is shared between the Centre and the states on 80: 20 ratio.

Employment Assurance Scheme (EAS)

The EAS was launched in 1993-94 for creating additional employment in rural areas for rural poor. EAS is quite similar to JRY except that it offers an assurance of 100 days employment (unskilled manual work) on minimum wage upto two members of a family in the age group of 18 to 60 years to all those rural poor who seek employment in the lean agro season.

Sampoorna Grameena Rozagar Yojana (SGRY)

The ministry of rural development reviewed Employment Assurance Scheme (EAS), (the only additional wage employment scheme for rural areas) and the Jawahar Gram Samridhi Yojana (JGSY) (a rural infrastructure development scheme) and merged them together to form Sampoorna Grameen Rozgar Yojana (SGRY) w.e.f. 25th September, 2001.

The primary objective of the Sampoorna Grameen Rozgar Yojana is to provide additional and supplementary wage employment and thereby provide food security and improve nutritional levels in all the rural areas. The secondary objective is the creation of durable community, social and economic assets and infrastructural development in rural areas.

The situation of employment is worse for rural areas, which accounts for 74 per cent of India's unemployed population. Despite low unemployment rates, the incidence of income poverty in rural areas is at least four times the incidence of unemployment as per the current daily status, which implies that the number of poor far outweighs the number of poor for want of work (Kannan, 2005). This, in other words, implies that the quality of employment is so low that the wage rate is inadequate to take care of even the limited notion of income poverty. In order to deal with unemployment problem in rural areas, Government of India, since independence has launched many employment programmes. A few important among them are:

Table 2.1: Wage Employment Programmes

Programmes	***Period***	***Objectives***
Rural Manpower Programme	1960-1969	Provide employment to 2.5 million persons in areas exposed to pronounced seasonal employment
Cash scheme for rural employment (CSRE)	1971-1974	Provide employment to 1000 persons in 350 districts through labour intensive works and create durable assets.
Drought Prone Areas Programme (DPAP), Rural works programme (Later restructured as Area Development Programme)	1971-1975	Mitigate the severity of scarcity conditions by organising labour intensive and production oriented works so as to generate considerable employment
Food for Work Programme (FWP)	1977- 1980	(i) Generate gainful employment to a large number of unemployed and under employed persons, both men and women in the rural areas which will improve their incomes and consequently their nutritional levels, (ii) Create durable community assets and strengthen the rural infrastructure which will result in high production and better living standard in rural areas; and (iii) Utilise surplus foodgrains for development of human resources.
National Rural Employment Programme (NREP)	1980-1989	Generate additional gainful employment; create durable community assets; and raise nutritional standards of the poor
Rural Landless Employment Guarantee Programme (RLEGP)	1983-1989	Provide 100 days of employment to atleast one member of a landless house hold
Jawahar Rozgar Yojana (JRY)	1989-1999	Generate additional gainful employment for unemployed and under-employed persons, both men and women, in rural

(contd...)

		areas through creation of rural economic infrastructure, community and social assets, particularly, in favour of the poor and with an aim at improving quality of life in rural areas.
Employment Assurance Scheme (EAS)	1993-1999	Provide 100 days of assured employment to a person in 1752 backward blocks during lean agricultural periods in the form of manual work.
Food for Work Programme II	2000-2002	Augment food security through wage employment in drought affected rural areas.
Jawahar Gram Samridhi Yojana (JGSY)	1999-2001	Primary objective: Creation of demand driven community village infrastructure, including (i) durable assets at the village level and (ii) assets to enable the rural poor to increase the opportunities for sustained employment ; secondary objective: Generation of supplementary employment for unemployed poor (Below Poverty Line) in the rural areas.
Sampoorna Grameen Rozgar Yojana (SGRY)	2001	Provide wage employment, food security, and creation of durable assets (the scheme was formed by merging EAS and JGSY)
Mahatma Gandhi National Rural Employment Guarantee Act (MGNREGA)	2005	- enhance livelihood security in rural areas by providing atleast 100 days of guaranteed wage employment in a financial year to every household whose adult members volunteer to do unskilled manual work - Generating productive assets, - Protecting the environment, - Empowering rural women, - Reducing rural urban immigration and - Fostering Social Equity.

Modified and Extracted from Drought 2002, Department of Agriculture and Cooperation, Ministry of Agriculture, GOI.

The Mahatma Gandhi National Rural Employment Guarantee Act

The National Rural Employment Guarantee Act, 2005 was enacted by Ministry of Rural Development (Govt. of India) to guarantee 100 days of employment in a financial year to any rural household whose adult members are willing to do unskilled manual work. The act came into force initially in 200 districts of the country to be gradually extended to other areas to be notified by the Central Government. The basic objective of the Act is to enhance livelihood security in rural areas by providing atleast 100 days of guaranteed wage employment in a financial year to every household whose adult members volunteer to do unskilled manual work. The other objectives that can be served by the Act are:

- Generating productive assets,
- Protecting the environment,
- Empowering rural women,
- Reducing rural urban immigration and
- Fostering Social Equity.

Works permissible under MGNREGA

As per the Schedule I of the Act, the focus of the Rural Employment Guarantee Scheme (REGS) shall be on the following works:

(i) Water conservation and water harvesting,

(ii) Drought proofing, including afforestation and tree plantation,

(iii) Irrigation from canals, including micro and minor irrigation works,

(iv) Provision of irrigation facility to land owned by households belonging to the SC/ST or to land of the beneficiaries of land reforms or to land of the beneficiaries under the Indira Awas Yojana,

(v) Renovation of traditional water bodies, including de-silting of tanks,

(vi) Land development,

(vii) Flood-control and protection works, including drainage in waterlogged areas.

(viii) Rural connectivity to provide all-weather access. The construction of roads may include culverts where ever necessary and within the village area along with drains and

(ix) Any other work that may be notified by the Central Government in consultation with the State Government.

***Features of the Scheme*:** MGNREGA provides 100 days of employment (unskilled, manual work) to all rural households on a self-selection basis and is cognisant of existing social inequalities that lead to the exclusion from economic growth opportunities of women and marginalised castes and ethnic groups, as identified in the Eleventh Five-Year Plan (Planning Commission, 2008). Nationally, over 40 million households have taken up MGNREGA employment. Almost 50 per cent of workers are women, 30 per cent of households belong to Scheduled Castes (SCs) and over 20 per cent belong to Scheduled Tribes (STs). Assets created through MGNREGA employment are based on local demand on both community and individually owned land: an important priority of the act is the opportunity to improve the productivity of land owned by households belonging to SC/STs, of that of the beneficiaries of land reforms and of land of below poverty line (BPL) families in the *Indira Awas Yojana* house construction programme (Ministry of Rural Development, 2008).

Comprehensive review of literature provides proper background information to design the research programme, analyse the research data and to interpret the research findings. Keeping in view the objectives, an effort was made to collect the literature related to the present study. Since MGNREGA is the flagship programme launched by the government to curtail unemployment and mostly respondents in the study got employed through this Scheme hence, this scheme becomes the focus of our assessing the socioeconomic profile of the respondents in the study area. Although a number of studies are conducted on MGNREGA with regard to general rural population but none on MGNREGA regarding Taungya community so a related review of literature was conducted. Furthermore, since MGNREGA was implemented in 2006, therefore, review of literature includes studies conducted after 2007, which limited the number of studies.

In this chapter, it was attempted to give the theoretical related review of literature of MGNREGA among the marginalised communities (SC, ST and women) as follows:

Pattanaik (2007) in his study 'NREGS: A micro appraisal of equity and efficiency has intensely analysed the implementation of NREGS and associated equity and efficiency issued in the Hoshiarpur District of Punjab. The findings of the study are based on the primary data collected from 10 village panchayats of two blocks in Mahilpur and Dasua of Hoshiarpur. The empirical findings of the study concerning efficiency issue indicates that the implementers of the scheme have failed to fulfill the promises ensured by the scheme. Furthermore Paucity of funds in mainly responsible for this lapse. The findings regarding Equity issues are more fulfilling. As per the empirical findings of the study, the disadvantaged section of society availed the flow of fund. The empirical findings emphasise on promotion of gender equity.

Centre for Science and Environment, 'An Assessment of the Performance of the National Rural Employment Guarantee Programme in Terms of its Potential for Creation of Natural Wealth in India's Villages', 2008. The Objectives of the study were to assess the potential impact of NREGA on the creation of natural resource asset base and the resultant impact of rural livelihood, food security, lifestyle changes, economic regeneration and impact on rural-urban migration. The Methodology involved using primary data collected from two districts, Nuapada district in Orissa and Sidhi district in Madhya Pradesh, the potential of the NREGA in providing food and livelihood security was assessed. The survey instrument that was developed contained detailed village and household level questionnaires called the Productive Asset Creation and Assessment Survey Tool (PACAST) to collect information on various aspects related to the implementation of NREGA. A random sample of 30 households per village was chosen from these villages for the household survey. The Findings were that under the NREGA, water conservation works are being taken up as stand-alone activities. Poor maintenance and weak institutions are already rendering productive assets useless. Under the current implementation regime, maintenance is not covered. While assets are created in large number, the Panchayats are being told to maintain it.

Khan, A. U *et al* (2008). This analysis looks at the direct and indirect effects that the NREGA has on employment generation and poverty reduction in a local. For this, a detailed survey in a specific village was undertaken to highlight the impact of the NREGP. This survey covered a poor agricultural village with 400 households and nearly 2,500 people. The survey recorded income and expenditure levels by type of household (large, small and marginal farmers, agricultural labour, services, etc.). The study shows that the sectors that show the maximum impact are wheat, animal husbandry, and education and the maximum impact on the household incomes accrues to the small cultivator followed by the labour household and then the large farmer households.

Pankaj, A. K *et al* (2008). This is a study of: (i) the implementation process, mechanism, difficulties and; (ii) impact of the scheme on the beneficiaries and communities vis-à-vis major objectives of the Act. The study is based on field work (survey) of nine districts (six from Bihar and three from Jharkhand), 30 villages (18 from Bihar and 12 from Jharkhand), 900 households, two-thirds beneficiaries and one-third non-beneficiaries (540 from Bihar and 360 from Jharkhand) and 37 worksites. This was also a resurvey of 102 beneficiary households in Bihar. This study examines the impact of the scheme on individual beneficiaries in terms of income consumption effects, changes in migration and indebtedness and impact of the community assets on the local economy, wage rate and agrarian conditions.

A study conducted by Ministry of Rural Development (2009) in District Purulia West Bengal shows that a Bandh is being excavated. Before this, the labourers found it difficult to get work locally and survived on the sale of firewood from which they earned approximately ₹ 15-20 per day. Through NREGA work, they have been able to earn nearly ₹ 65-70 per day based on the quantum of work done.

Khera *et al* (2009) in the findings of the survey states that the participation of women in the NREGA was below the stipulated minimum 33 per cent. U.P. and Bihar were at the bottom with women accounting for only 5 and 13 per cent of NREGA workforce, situation is marginally better in Jharkhand (18 per cent) and Chhattisgarh (25 per cent). The only states where women were well represented were Madhya Pradesh (44 per cent) and Rajasthan (71 per cent).

Ramesh *et al* (2009) emphasised on a study conducted in Karimnagar district Andhra Pradesh by selecting 500 women beneficiaries of NREGA. The findings of the study reveal that 51.6 per cent of workers are from Backward community and 46.6 per cent of workers are from SC category. As far as age-wise distribution is concerned, 39 per cent of workers are in 30-40 years age group. Thirty-five per cent in 20-30 years age group and the rest of them in 40-50 years age group. This shows that majority of the workers are below 40 years of age.

Dutta (2009) in the article 'NREGA in West Bengal' Success and challenges' conducted a study in North 24 Parganas with higher concentration of BPL families. The finding depict that there is an increase mandays, employment created durable assets and strengthened infrastructure. Distress migration has reduced.

Barna Maullick (2009) stressed that majority of the beneficiary workers were in the age group of 18-35 years. The beneficiaries come from scheduled castes households, women participation is very low, material cost is on higher side and average day of employment is one fifth of the specified days i.e. 22 days against 100 days and there has been no involvement of the contractor and the machines in the works related to the schemes.

Central Institute of Fisheries Education (CIFE), (2009). The study undertook an assessment of MGNREGA in two districts of Maharashtra, Thane and Akola. The findings included significant representation of women and SCs and STs in MGNREGA works, increased employment opportunities, etc. The constraints identified were unemployment allowance not paid, delay in wage payments, lack of worksite facilities, etc.

Hazarika, P. G. (2009). The primary objective of this research is to study the impact of the National Rural Employment Guarantee Programme on women's empowerment and gender inequality and to identify major constraints, if any, on their access to productive employment opportunities through the employment guarantee programme. This study is basically the outcome of the researcher's field work in Assam. The essay focuses on women workers in two selected districts of the State, to derive conclusions to highlight the impact of the programme on the lives of women workers and gender relations. Significant findings reported by the study include, income gain, social empowerment, more say in intra-household decision-making and creation of community assets, etc. The study concludes by identifying certain barriers to women's access to MGNREGA and important learning lessons for policy.

Khera, R., *et al.*, (2009). This paper, based on fieldwork in six States in 2008, examines the socio-economic consequences of the NREGA for women workers. In spite of the drawbacks in the implementation of the legislation, significant benefits have already started accruing to women through better access to local employment, at minimum wages, with relatively decent and safe work conditions. The paper also discusses barriers to women's participation.

Nair, K. N *et al* (2009). This paper attempts to study the impact of the NREG in three GPs of Kasaragod District, viz. Madikai, Ajanoor and Trikarpur. The positive findings are that all those who demanded jobs have been given employment. The percentage of man-days generated for SC and ST categories is very low compared to that of the general category. Women of the general category constituted the major beneficiaries of NREGA. Unskilled wages constituted the major component of expenditure. The number of projects is large, most of them not leading to creation of durable public assets.

Dheeraja, C., *et al*, (2010). This is a study on the impact of MGNREGS on gender relations in 102 districts in 27 States. The study found that gender relations in favour of women increased in the post-MGNREGS period. Self-esteem, self-image and confidence levels of women improved through their participation under MGNREGS. SHGs contributed to the changes in gender relations among the members and MGNREGS consolidated these changes. Gender Relation Index (GRI) consisting of social, economic and political dimensions at both household and community levels increased for women after implementation of MGNREGS.

Institute of Rural Management Anand (IRMA), (2010). The methodology followed was multipronged mixed methodology approach. Stratified random sampling was followed along with extensive case studies of MGNREGA implementation. The Findings of the study were that under MGNREGA, four major types of work were implemented: water conservation, Land development, Plantation and afforestation and Road connectivity. In order to enhance rural water security, the state had initiated a new spring shed development programme jointly with people's science institute, Dehradun and WWF India under the banner of 'MGNREGA Dhara Vikas'-outcome of this initiative include preparation of a 'village spring atlas' and increase in the discharge of the springs (recommended for my Thesis). MGNREGA has provided a source of supplementary income to the families without making any wage discrimination between men and women, hence it is the local women who are the active participants under this scheme. MGNREGA has led to enhanced empowerment of women providing them with a common platform to discuss issues and awareness generation. The Gaps identified were Durability and sustainability of assets created under MGNREGA was absent.

Samarthan, (2010) conducted a study in 16 districts in Madhya Pradesh. The study sample was split across different geographical areas, phases of implementation, their performance on employment generation and also different categories of households. Some of the key findings of the report include, low awareness levels among beneficiaries, no clear strategy for maintenance of assets and funds to be used for maintenance and social audits not being conducted. In the cases where social audits were conducted the issues of less wage payment (69 per cent), quality and use of work (75.5 per cent), work demands (75.5 per cent) have figured prominently. On the positive side, the largest proportion of estimated benefited households spend their MGNREGA income on food, medicine, and clothes for the family members, i.e. 81 per cent, 55 per cent, 41 per cent respectively.

Shah, T. *et al*, (2010). This report synthesises insights from 40 case studies of MGNREGS works undertaken by the students of Institute of Rural Management (IRMA) across 11 districts in nine States during 2009–10. In general, the study found, (i) workseekers as well as the rest of the village community were adequately prepared for deriving Scheme's benefits; (ii) village power structures wanted to use MGNREGS to build broad-based political capital; (iii) the core and spirit of the MGNREGA protocol were upheld and the panchayat and block-administration played their respective roles adequately; and (iv) what MGNREGA offers has a good 'fit' with what work-seekers, village community and local leadership want.

Dasgupta, S. *et al*, (2011). Using data from the 2004–05 NSSO survey and NREGA data from official sites, the study finds that: (i) women's participation in the NREGA has been increasing; (ii) statewise women's participation in the programme is positively correlated with women's participation in rural areas, though women's participation in NREGA is often higher than in other forms of recorded work so far; and (iii) women's participation is negatively correlated with the existing gender wage gap in unskilled agricultural labour. The latter implies that where women's actual wages as a share of men's is lower in the private sector, women are flocking to work in this government administered programme. This will inevitably raise women's bargaining power, and is potentially a critical factor in reducing gender disparities in the labour market.

Sinha, R. K. *et al*, (2011). in a study makes an assessment of MGNREGA with respect to the extent of employment generation, wage differentials, rural to urban migration, asset creation, determinants of participation and implementation in five districts of Bihar. The report suggests that MGNREGA succeeded in terms of reducing migration of labourers but only to a low extent. Wage differentials also reduced after implementation. General wage rate for male and female in both farm and non-farm activities increased. For assets, the performance of projects completed and total amount spent on works under MGNREGA during the reference years in all the selected districts were more or less satisfactory and emboldening for the job-seeking poor people of the rural area.

Vaidya, C. S *et al,* (2011).The study makes an assessment of MGNREGA with respect to the extent of employment generation, wage differentials, rural to urban migration, asset creation, determinants of participation and implementation in five districts of Himachal Pradesh. The main findings of the study suggested that out-migration was mainly the result of higher wages prevailing in the nearby towns; MGNREGA enhanced food security, provided protection against extreme poverty, helped to reduce distress migration and indebtedness and gave greater economic independence to women and purchasing power to the local economy. In terms of work, majority of the respondents found that there were good quality assets created under MGNREGA.

Vatta, K. *et al*., (2011). In the paper makes an assessment of MGNREGA with respect to the extent of employment generation, its effect on rural to urban migration, asset creation, determinants of participation and implementation in Punjab. Primary data was collected from 300 households in five districts of the State where the Scheme was implemented in different phases. It was found that family size, asset value, household income and stage of implementation of MGNREGA were significant indicators of household participation. At the worker level age and education were not found to be significant for participation. The wages of casual labour have increased due to an overall decline in the supply of labour to the agriculture sector. These changes have been the reason for the significant decline in the inflow of labour into Punjab. Keeping in mind the present number of job-seekers and their future growth, the employment opportunities under MGNREGA have to be increased by almost 11 times in Punjab.

Verma, S., (2011). Data from a study of 140+ best-performing MGNREGS water assets in 75 villages across eight districts of Bihar, Gujarat, Kerala and Rajasthan shows that, on an average, these assets were able to recover their investments in a little over a year. The study also found that MGNREGS implementation deeply influences and is, in turn, influenced by the farm and non-farm labour markets. While the wage-benefits of MGNREGS are clear from the data on number of person-days of employment generated, the quantification of non-wage benefits and their distribution requires deeper investigation.

Asha Sharma, (2012). The purpose of the paper is to highlight the difference in employment and empowerment attainment among the SC/ST women in rural India.The Design/methodology/approach of the paper uses data from the Centre for Science and Environment: NREGA Implementation Status, Jan 2008 update: http://www/cseindia.org/programme/nrml/update_january08.htm#NREGA and Centre for development studies- Thiruvananthapuram. The Findings are the high status of women among the SC/ST groups in the Rajnandgoan, Jhabua, Mayurbhanj and Cuddalore has important effect on the generating community assets and enhancing their spending capacity. High poverty rates pose to be significant obstacles in attaining empowerment among SC/ST women in rural India. By putting cash earning in women's hands, NREGA has both increased and diversified the contribution that women are making to household incomes as wage earners.The suggestions were that difference in economic, social, and cultural background among the various SC/ST women in rural India need to be emphasised in order to understand the importance of MGNREGA.

Hirway, I., *et al.*, (2012). This study by Indira Hirway reveals that MGNREGA has also added to women's time burden and drudgery. Much is yet to be done in empowering women to become active participants as well as real beneficiaries of MGNREGA. This study highlights the impact of MGNREGA on women in the village of Movasa, Gujarat.

Verma, S., (2012). MGNREGS deeply influences and is, in turn, influenced by the rural farm and non-farm labour markets. In 2009–10 and then again 2010–11, IWMI deployed more than 50 masters students from the Institute of Rural Management, Anand (IRMA) to understand how MGNREGA and village labour markets interact. The students covered 26 villages in 11 districts of nine States in 2009 and 13 villages in 11 districts of nine states in 2010. In addition, eight IRMA students surveyed village leaders, labourers and farmers in 75 villages from Gujarat, Rajasthan, Bihar and Kerala. This note synthesises and summarises the lessons from these field studies.

Srinivasa Rao Didde1, *et al*, (2013). The objective of the paper is to examine the extent to which the intended programme has reached the tribals people in terms of employment generation, asset creation and wage accruals through involving MGNREGA works for the last five years of the programme at the village level in Parvathipuram Integrated Tribal Development Agency (ITDA), Parvathipuram Mandal, Budurvada village. This is located in Vizianagaram district, Andhra Pradesh. This is a higher tribal participating village in Parvathipuram Mandal under the MGNREGA. The reference period for the analysis is from 2006-07 to 2010-11. The data is collected from secondary sources for this study it includes the information available on the official websites of MGNREGA and APNREGA. Simple averages, ratios, and percentages have been used to carry out my objective. The major findings of the study are no household in tribal of the village completed 100 days employment in first three years of the programme, above 50 per cent employment sharing by the tribal women in every year in this village.

Sourav Das, "*Performance of Mahatma Gandhi National Rural Employment Guarantee Scheme with Special Reference to Hugli District of West Bengal*", 2013, In this paper an attempt has been made to focus some lights on the measures of performance of MGNREGS in Hugli district of West Bengal. This paper investigates the status of MGNREGS in Hugli district after the implementation of the programme. However, the paper finds interblock variation in some important indicators like average person days generated per household, the proportion of works completed to works taken up and the proportion of local fund spent.

Rituparna Bhattacharyya. *et al*, (2013). This research is an attempt to examine the participation of women in MGNREGA, Assam. It critically looks at the issues, problems and challenges confronted by the women while working at MGNREGA. Written from a feminist perspective on gender, poverty and women's empowerment, the research seeks to address the problems of the women beneficiaries through their lived experiences. For this, we conducted in-depth interviews with the women beneficiaries in the months of August and September, 2009 in four remote areas namely, Burka, Chandrapur, Barbhang and Muguriya, the first two situated in Kamrup, while the third and the fourth in Barpeta districts of Assam, where the programme of MGNREGA is on-going. The findings of the research suggest measures so that the programme can be made more effective in the long run.

Chapter - 3

Impact of Wage Employment Scheme on Village Development

This chapter emphasises on overall development of the villages, inhabited by the Taungya population, due to wage employment schemes like MGNREGA. Since MGNREGA is a scheme which is most prevalent in this area so it becomes imperative to assess the impact of the sustainability aspect of this scheme through assessment of overall development of the village. The impact of MGNREGA on the development of village has been assessed through the following ways:

1. Assets created under the MGNREGA works in the village.
2. MGNREGA Process implementation assessment based on beneficiaries perceptions through SWOT analysis.

This objective presents the details of various works carried out as part of soil and water conservation measures and improving rural connectivity. The study also throws light on the scheme implementation, problems faced by the community and remedial measures that can be thought of. The observations have been made on the process of execution and quality of work for resource improvement at individual and community level. The findings of the assessment are contributing in terms of specific recommendation and suggestions for overall improvement in technical intervention so that the provisions under MGNREGA should not limit only up to employment creation scheme, but people should look beyond as sustainable livelihood support system.

Assets Created Under the MGNREGA Works in the Village

Box below shows that the respondents participated in the execution of seven types of MGNREGA works: Rural connectivity, road maintenance, drainage construction and/or maintenance, Drought proofing, water conservation and water harvesting, land development and afforestation. Similarly, several of the respondents participated in a combination of at least two of these types of work MGNREGA works happening in the selected blocks/villages:

Box 3.1: The Permissible works conducted under MGNREGA in the Study Area

Districts	*Blocks*	*Villages*	*Works*
Saharanpur	Muzaffarabad	Karaundi Khushalpur Ganeshpur Panchayat Kaluwala	Kharonza nirman, Miti karya, Rural connectivity Drought proofing, Flood control and protection, Rural connectivity Rural connectivity, Afforestation Plantation work, Drought proofing Rural connectivity, Water conservation and water harvesting, Other works
Dehradun	Sahaspur Vikasnagar	Bhagwatpur Timli	Flood control and protection, Water conservation and water harvesting Water conservation and water harvesting

Source: Fieldwork returns.

Fig. 3.1: **Mitti Murram** *works.*

Table 3.1: Details of the MGNREGA works carried in the Study Area

Villages	***Works***	***Year***	***Projects***	***Status***	***Owner***
Karaundi	*Kharonza nirman* *Miti karya*	2011 2011 2012	2 3 2	Completed Completed Ongoing	*Fulsingh ke khet se Ramesh ke khet tak mitti karya* *Karondi me pakki sadak se manu ke khet tak*
Khushalpur	*Kharonza nirman* *Mitti karya* Plantation works	2011 2011 2011 2012	4 1 7 7	Completed Completed Completed	*Khushalipur me puliya se matlub ke ghar tak mitti* *Khajnawer 2 beet me plantation* *Khushalpur farm me plantation* *Sarwajanik bhoomi par warsharopan*
Ganeshpur Panchayat	Rural connectivity *Kharonza nirman* Afforestation	2010 2011 2011 2011	2 1 11 8	Completed Ongoing Completed Completed	Ganeshpur- mohand road maintenance *Ganeshpur se mohand marg* *Pushta nirman* *Wrakhsharopan,* *Gov.Resham farm* *Ganeshpur me planting karya,* Kajnawer 2B ANR ANU.
Kaluwala	Drought proofing *Mitti Karya* Water conservation and water harvesting	2011 2011 2012 2011	16 4 2 9	Completed Completed Completed Completed	*Puliya nirman* *Gov Resham farm* *JahanpurI me mitti karya.* *Dudhla talab se jangal tak mitti karya.* *Gov Resham farm* *JahanpurII me med bandi aur Nali nirman.*
Bhagwatpur	Flood control and protection Water conservation and water harvesting	2012 2013	1 3	Completed Ongoing	
Timli	Water conservation and water harvesting	2013	2	Ongoing	

Source: Primary data, 2014.

Table 3.1 shows that the majority of the respondents participated in work proceeded under the MGNREGA either related to road maintenance, afforestation or drainage construction and/or maintenance.

These were roads connecting the villages of Ganeshpur-Mohand road maintenance and construction of *Ganeshpur se mohand marg*. Other works carried out regarding rural connectivity were Mitti Murram roads like *Fulsingh ke khet se Ramesh ke khet tak mitti karya* and *Karondi me pakki sadak se manu ke khet tak*. Three sites were visited in three villages to assess the Mitti Murrum road construction under MGNREGA. All three schemes were completed. The Murrum is not applied on the track that has already completed the earth work. It has also been noted that the proper dressing of the side slopes and compaction of the road is not given due attention. This would result in early damage to the road. During the site visits, it was noticed that at many places there is a need of crossways and culverts, however, the provision for the same is not under MGNREGA, as informed by *Panchayat Sevaks*. It has been observed at many places, that there was no provision to drain out the excess water near the roads. As a result there was damage to the road and adjoining areas.

***Fig. 3.2: Checkdams constructed near Gujjar* khol.**

Fig. 3.3: Checkdams constructed near Taungya village.

Fig. 3.4: Pond constructed under MGNREGA works.

Under the water harvesting and water conservation works, check dams were constructed. Check Dams are permanent structures built across streams or gullies where other temporary and semi-permanent structures are ineffective due to the high quantity and velocity of runoff.

Check Dams are adoptable in streams of moderate slope/ lower reaches of the watershed basin for water harvesting. In the present appraisal study, two check dam sites were visited Kaluwala and Timli. The sites of the two completed Check Dams were visited and found in use presently.

Under water harvesting works, respondents also participated in pond construction. This pond was situated in a Taungya plantations leading to Timli khol. The workers removed mud and silt from the bottom of the pond and placed it on the sides to increase the pond's capacity to store rainwater.

In relation to the trough, nine per cent of the respondents participated in constructing it in the Taungya village. The purpose of the trough was to collect rainwater in a small pond for the residing cattle in a downward hillside, and it was constructed by bricks and cement. 21.8 per cent of the respondents participated in drainage construction and/or maintenance at Ganeshpur village. The nature of the work was the construction of new drainage systems or removal of sand, plants and waste from the drainage. Data in the previous chapter showed that 90 per cent of Taungya respondents participated in the afforestation works carried out by the Forest Department.

Fig. 3.5: Afforestation Works under MGNREGA.

In addition, 30 per cent Gujjar respondents participated in constructing the school compound in Pathrauli Gujjar khol. This can be seen in relation to a general lack of knowledge about the MGNREGA in the population, which made it difficult for several of the respondents to differentiate which work they participated in that came under the Act or not. Commonly, the working day lasted for nine hours between 8:00 am to 5:00 pm with a one hour lunch break.

MGNREGA Process Assessment Through Swot Analysis

SWOT analysis is a qualitative method for the strategic planning. SWOT represents Strengths, Weakness, Opportunity and Threat. SWOT analysis is used for situational analysis. Strengths are the basic assets of MGNREGA that helps in the growth and development of its beneficiaries. Weaknesses are the shortcomings of MGNREGA process implementation which leads to situation specific disadvantage to ultimate beneficiaries. Opportunities are the ability or capacity of the beneficiaries to utilise the MGNREGA scheme for their own development. Threats are the situations that may block the ability of MGNREGA to help its beneficiaries to grow and develop.

Table 3.2: Strengths of MGNREGA as perceived by Taungya Participants N=100

Strengths	*Mean*	*S D*
Taungya		
(i) Curtail migration	2.840	.370
(ii) Involved participation of women.	2.820	.388
(iii) Livelihood alleviation programme that promises relief stimulus	2.780	.418
(iv) Very successful programme that promises jobs to needy.	2.740	.527
(v) Development of village infrastructure	2.140	.404

Note: Scale values: -1-Not Important, 2- Moderately Important, 3-Highly Important.

The inspection ofTable 3.2 indicates that curtail migration (Mean= 2.840), involved participation of women (Mean= 2.820), livelihood alleviation programme that promises relief stimulus (Mean= 2.780), very successful programme that promises jobs to needy (Mean= 2.740) and development of village infrastructure (Mean= 2.140) were perceived as main strengths by Taungya respondents of MGNREGA. Participants perceive curtail migration (Mean= 2.840) as the topmost strength of MGNREGA in Taungya community. Since work is available within village proximity, women are not left alone in the forest area to attend to children alone. Parents are able to spend time with their children as they donot have to go to far off township for work. Involved participation of women (Mean= 2.820) was evident from 90 per cent Taungya women participation in MGNREGA workforce and its positive impact on the households have been discussed in the previous chapter. Livelihood alleviation programme that promises relief stimulus (Mean= 2.780) is perceived as strength of MGNREGA in Taungya community because MGNREGA has led to an enhanced access to social assets. This research suggested that there is a general perception that social networks are strengthened as a result of MGNREGA, leading to improved relationships where by men and women work together as well as supporting strengthening informal safety nets by borrowing small amounts from each other. One of the reasons cited for this was that, since the implementation of MGNREGA, people have been able to access credit from either their neighbours or their relatives as they have enhanced repayment assurance due to enhanced employment security.Very successful programme that promises jobs to needy (Mean= 2.740) was perceived as a strength as Taungya women find easy employment in the afforestation works started under MGNREGA nearer to their villages although the wages under MGNREGA are less than the wages at worksites. Development of village infrastructure is perceived as a strength as most of the MGNREGA works pertains to road construction, plantation works or construction of community assets like a well or school building.

Table 3.3: Weaknesses of MGNREGA as perceived by Taungya Participants

Weakness	*Mean*	*S D*
Taungya		
(i) Very poor knowledge/ awareness of MGNREGA act and benefits	2.800	.404
(ii) Expenditure oriented and not demand driven	2.780	.418
(iii) Very poor participation of people in deciding village needs	2.340	.688
(iv) Low worksite facilities	2.220	.418
(v) Worksites outside the villages	1.240	.431

Note: Scale values: - 1- Not Important, 2- Moderately Important, 3- Highly Important.

Inspection of the Table 3.3 indicates that very poor knowledge/ awareness of MGNREGA act and benefits (Mean=2.800), expenditure oriented and not demand driven (Mean=2.780), very poor participation of people in deciding village needs (Mean=2.340), low worksite facilities (Mean=2.220) and worksites outside the villages (Mean=1.240) were perceived as the major weaknesses of MGNREGA in Taungya community.Taungya workers are not aware of the provisions under the MGNREGA works and facilities to be made available on the worksites.Workers were never consulted in the nature of works to be carried out in the Gram Sabha meetings and were merely happy with the fact that works were being carried out nearer to their villages.

Table 3.4: Opportunities of MGNREGA as perceived by Participants

Opportunities	*Taungya*	
	Mean	*S D*
(i) Integrating river channels, rain water harvesting, desilting	2.960	.197
(ii) MGNREGA Programme can be redesigned to build or match Skill sets of that particular locality.	2.800	.404
(iii) Can focus more on livelihood enhancement programmes like Sanitation, drinking water facilitation.	2.780	.418
(iv) Enhancement of NGO participation.	2.020	.197
(v) Build on ecosystem that drives itself.	1.960	.282

Note: Scale values: - 1- Not Important, 2- Moderately Important, 3- Highly Important.

Important opportunities of MGNREGA as perceived by Taungya respondents shown in Table 3.4 were integrating river channels, rain water harvesting, desilting (Mean=2.960), MGNREGA Programme can be redesigned to build or match skill sets of that particular locality (Mean=2.800), can focus more on livelihood enhancement programmes like sanitation, drinking water facilitation (Mean= 2.780), enhancement of NGO participation (Mean=2.020) and building on ecosystem that drives itself (Mean=1.960). Taungya villages are in the Shivalik foothills where during summers, there is immense scarcity of water due to drying up of river. MGNREGA works can be carried out where the water harvesting systems can be devised out for these communities. MGNREGA Programme can be redesigned to build or match skill sets of that particular locality (Mean=2.800) is perceived as an opportunity by the respondents as these ethnic communities own their peculiar skill set of indigenous knowledges pertaining to livestock and natural resource management. Panchayats and Forest Department should assist MGNREGA beneficiaries with securing sustainable employment by introducing skill-development programmes, perhaps in tandem with current public works. Build on ecosystem that drives itself (Mean=1.960) is another opportunity as there is a real need of resource mapping and knowledge mapping to decide which part of the village needs what resources and to make sure the MGNREGA benefits reach the people who need them most. The important part of sustenance of these projects as an asset for the community is not planned.

Table 3.5: Threats of MGNREGA as perceived by Taungya Participants

Threats	*Taungya*	
	Mean	*SD*
(i) Panchayat need to develop a proactive mind set	2.960	.197
(ii) Government's approach of restricting the scope to 'Unskilled labour' work might be an hinderance to the Programme/developments in the long run.	2.960	.197
(iii) Delay in wage payment	2.160	.370

Note: Scale values: -1-Not Important, 2- Moderately Important, 3- Highly Important.

It gets evident from the Table 3.5 above that Panchayat need to develop a proactive mind set is perceived as the biggest threat by both these communities. There is a need to initiate programmes to train gram panchayat presidents and their staff in the basic skills required to effectively implement MGNREGA and equip gram panchayats with appropriate infrastructure, material resources, and technical and administrative personnel.

Government's approach of restricting the scope to 'unskilled labour' work might be an hinderance to the programme/developments in the long run. In addition to the types of assets that are being created under MGNREGA, there is also concern regarding the sustainability of the employment opportunities the programme offers. By relying on works derived from unskilled labour, MGNREGA projects are ultimately not contributing to the development of a productive workforce. A Taungya *pradhan* emphasised that MGNREGA will give

Taungyas some money, but it won't necessarily help them catch up. They are impoverished precisely because they are doing unskilled labour, not moving out of their situation and gaining new skills or capabilities.

Delay in wage payment is perceived as another threat as for the significant number of Taungya workers already living below subsistence level, failing to receive timely wages may lead individuals to migrate or to seek employment from contractors, under potentially exploitative conditions. The source of these wage delays is unclear. When asked how convenient it was for them to collect their wages, workers in one district reported that the nearest bank was ten kilometers away. In addition to enduring delays in wage payments, workers do not receive unemployment allowances. In fact, there is little evidence that workers in UP recognise their right to demand work. From observations on the fieldwork, it appears that work is entirely supply-driven, with participants receiving work according to the whim of the gram panchayat president.

Constraints Faced by Taungya Participants of MGNREGA

The constraints being faced by the beneficiaries have been presented in Table. Most of the beneficiaries (42 per cent) reported that the delay in wage payment as the prime constraint, followed by the process of payment of wages through banks or post offices was stated as a hectic process by 42 per cent of the respondents. Long queues on the days of wage payment, and the process of filling the forms for the illiterate workers were the other difficulties associated with bank or post office payments. According to some of the respondents, it spoils a working day. Other constraints cited by the beneficiaries were non-availability of regular work (28 per cent), corruption (18 per cent) and lack of special provision for the old persons (18 per cent). Most of the beneficiaries in particular women complained of non-availability of work site facility (16 per cent). No provision for skilled or semi-skilled works (14 per cent) was another issue cited by the beneficiaries.

One of a problem with MGNREGA is the negative social impact as a jobcard is issued to a household and 100 days of employment is provided against a jobcard. A dangerous trend identified was that young sons were leaving their old parents and establishing a new family and the old persons were facing many problems.

Table 3.6: Constraints being Faced by Sample Participants (n=100)

Constraint	*Taungya*
Delay in wage payment	20
Non-availability of regular work	10
No special provisions for elderly persons	10
Hectic process of Bank/ Post Office payments	28
Corruption	10
Non-availability of work site facility	10
Some works not of good quality and necessity	4
Jobcards not working regularly	4
No provision for skilled or semi-skilled	4

Figures within the parentheses indicate percentage to sample of beneficiaries.

The other constraints associated with the programme were existence of corruption at many levels (18 per cent) and no provision for skilled or semi-skilled works was pointed out by 14 per cent of them. About six per cent reported very exhaustive manual labour and some respondents complained that some of the works done under MGNREGS were not of good quality and were not necessary (six per cent).

Chapter - 4

Socio-economic Development of Taungya due to Wage Employment

In Uttarakhand, the NREGA was initially launched in three districts i.e., Chamoli, Champawat and Tehri in 2006-07 (Phase-1). In second phase (2007-08), two additional districts, i.e., Haridwar and Udhamsingh Nagar were added. In the last phase, all the remaining districts have been notified under the NREGS. The Act also seeks to create durable assets to augment land and water resources, improve rural connectivity and strengthen the basic needs of the rural poor. MGNREGA works are largely focused on land and water resources which include: water harvesting and conservation, soil conservation and protection, irrigation provisioning and improvement, renovation of traditional water bodies, land development and drought proofing. These MGNREGA have the potential to generate environmental benefits such as ground recharge, soil and water conservation, drought and floods.

In order to assess the impact of MGNREGA Scheme in the Taungya villages, a purposive sampling technique was implied to collect the data through an Interview Schedule. A data set with a sample size of 100 households was collected from three Taungya villages. Out of these 100 households, 50 households were purposively selected of the respondents who were participating in the works of MGNREGA and have been referred as Participant Taungya throughout the study. On the other hand, another sample size of 50 households was selected from the respondents who were not participating in MGNREGA and this set of respondents were referred as Non participant Taungya throughout the study.

Demographic Profile of the Taungya Respondents

Age

It is clear from the Table 4.1 that 50 per cent of Taungyas participating in MGNREGA were in the age bracket 31-45 years, 20 per cent were in the age bracket upto 30 years and 30 per cent in above 45 years of age. Among the nonparticipant Taungyas, 28 per cent of the respondents were in the age bracket of above 45 years while 20 per cent were in the age bracket of upto 30 years and 52 per cent were in the age bracket of 31-45 years.

The age distribution shows that majority of participant Taungya respondents were in the age bracket 31-45 years so the young Taungyas mostly opted for MGNREGA works.

Gender

Table 4.1 explains the sex-wise distribution of the sample respondents. Out of the total Taungya participants, 10 per cent were male respondents and 90 per cent were the female participants.

Table 4.1: Demographic Profile of Participant and Nonparticipant Taungya

		Participants	*Non Participants*	*Total*
	Age			
(i)	Upto 30 years	10(20)	10(20)	**20**
(ii)	31-45 years	25(50)	26(52)	**51**
(iii)	Above 45 years	15(30)	14(28)	**29**
	Total	**50(100)**	**50(100)**	**100**
	Gender			
(i)	Male	05(10)	25(50)	**30**
(ii)	Female	45(90)	25(50)	**70**
	Total	**50 (100)**	**50 (100)**	**100**
	Family Type			
(i)	Nuclear	44(88)	45(90)	**89**
(ii)	Joint	6(12)	5(10)	**11**
	Total	**50(100)**	**50(100)**	**100**

Figures in parenthesis show percentages to their respective totals.

Data showed that in Taungya community more of females participated in MGNREGA than the male force who migrated to adjoining townships for labour works.

Family Type

It is clear from the Table 4.1 that 88 per cent of participant Taungya were from nuclear family and 12 per cent were from joint family. On the other hand, 10 per cent of nonparticipant Taungya were from joint family and 90 per cent were from nuclear family.

Field observations showed that amongst the Taungya community, nuclear family system is a norm of the society and as soon as the son gets married, he is expected to support his own family. The reason cited mostly by them is that they have meagre resources in terms of land and livestock to depend on for their livelihood so their occupational pattern is mostly labour works and afforestation activities. This occupational pattern makes it feasible for them to sustain a small family.

Family Size

The above Table 4.1 explains that 50 per cent of participant Taungya households have a family size of upto five members with an average family size of four, 44 per cent have a family size of 5-10 members with an average family size of seven and six per cent have a family size of more than 10 members with an average family size of 10. On the other hand, 30 per cent of non-participant Taungya households have a family size of upto five members with an average family size of four, 68 per cent have a family size of 5-10 members with an average family size of seven and two per cent have a family size of more than 10 members with an average family size of 16.

Table 4.2: Distribution of sample households according to Family Size in Taungya Community

Family size	*Participants*		*Nonparticipant*		*Pooled*	
	No.	*Average Size*	*No.*	*Average Size*	*No.*	*Average Size*
5 Members	25(50)	4	15(30)	4	40	4
5-10 Members	22(44)	7	34(68)	7	56	7
More than 10 Members	3(6)	10	1(2)	16	4	13
Total	**50**	**6**	**50**	**6**	**100**	**6**

Figures in parenthesis show percentages to their respective totals.

It was observed that Taungya people have small families as education is more prevalent amongst Taungyas and most of them are aware of the benefits of having smaller families emphasising on the quality of life that they can give to their children which is possible only if they have less number of children.

Table 4.3: Social Profile of Taungya Respondents

		Participants Taungya	*Non-Participants Taungya*	*Total*
	Levels of Education			
(i)	Illiterate	0	2(4)	2
(ii)	Can read and write	1(2)	10 (20)	11
(iii)	Primary	49 (98)	38 (76)	87
	Total	**50(100)**	**50(100)**	**100**
	Reasons for educational drop out			
(i)	Economic	44(78)	40 (80)	84
(ii)	Personal	06	10 (20)	16
	Total	**50 (100)**	**50 (100)**	**100**
	Sources of treatment of Taungya			
(i)	Family member	0	10 (20)	10
(ii)	Local *Vaidya*	10 (20)	10 (20)	40
(iii)	Doctor	40 (80)	30 (60)	50
	Total	**50**	**50**	**100**
	Urban contact			
(i)	Weekly	43 (86)	15 (30)	15
(ii)	Daily	7 (14)	35 (70)	85
	Total	**50**	**50**	**100**
	Occupation			
(i)	Wages	0	24 (48)	24
(ii)	MGNREGAWage+Livestock	7 (14)	0	7
(iii)	Wage+farming	0	6 (12)	6
(iv)	MGNREGA+forest works	43 (86)	0	43
(v)	Wages + Baan-making	0	20 (40)	20
	Total	**50**	**50**	**100**

Figures in parenthesis show percentages to their respective totals.

Social Development Profile and Impact of MGNREGA on Taungya

Social Impact of Taungya Community has been assessed on the basis of:

(i) Education level;

(ii) Health Profile;

(iii) Urban Contacts;

(iv) Occupation pattern.

Educational Profile

From the data in Table 4.3, 98 per cent of Taungya participants had primary education and 2 per cent were neoliterates. Among the non-participant Taungyas, 76 per cent were educated till primary level, 20 per cent were neoliterates and 4 per cent were illiterate. This shows 87 per cent of levels of primary education among Taungyas which is reasonably high. The reasons cited by them for their educational dropout were low income levels (78 per cent). After the stoppage of Taungya system in the year 1974, the families were left with meagre one acre of land to cultivate but the dry spells during summers and with no irrigation facilities, it became difficult for them to cultivate their fields. Due to poverty, most of them started working at an early age resulting in low levels of education.

Field observations showed that the higher literacy levels upto primary level of education is due to the underlying reason of an establishment of a primary school within 1 km of proximity of a Taungya village as a provision within the Taungya settlement plan. Although the primary education is available which makes them literate however, the quality of the educational knowledge remains questionable. Further more, as almost all the houses are one room tenements, children donot get proper study space. However, for secondary education they need to go to a distant township which is nearest at 10-12 kms away and since there is no transportation facility for nearly 5 kms near to their village, most of the Taungya people dropout after primary education although the desire for further education is there amongst them.

Health Profile of Taungya Respondents

Source of Treatment

As discussed in the Table 4.3, 80 per cent of participants Taungya got treated by private doctors and 20 per cent went to local *vaidya* for treatment. A total of 60 per cent of non participant Taungya went to

Table 4.4: Health profile of Taungya Respondents

		Participant Taungya	*Non-Participant Taungya*	*Total*	*Difference*
	Place of Delivery and assistance during Delivery in Taungya				
(i)	Institutional Delivery	7(14)	1(2)	8	+12%
(ii)	Home Delivery	30(60)	40(80)	70	-20%
(iii)	Assisted by nurse/midwife	10(20)	1(2)	7	+18%
(iv)	Assisted by relatives	3(6)	8(16)	11	-10%
	Total	**50(100)**	**50(100)**	**100**	
	Antenatal and Post natal care among Taungya women				
(i)	Antenatal checkups	5(10)	15(30)	20	-20%
(ii)	IFA tablets and TT immunization	35(70)	25(50)	60	+20%
(iii)	Post natal checkup	10(20)	10(20)	20	
	Total	**50**	**50**	**100**	
	Immunization status of 0-5 years Children Among Taungya				
(i)	Children *0-10years	26(52)	3(6)	29 (49)	
(ii)	None	-		31(51)	
	Total			**60(100)**	
	Use of Different family planning methods by Taungya eligible couples				
(i)	Sterilisation	6(12)	8(16)	14	-4%
(ii)	IUCD	10(20)	2(4)	12	+16%
(iii)	Oral pills	12(24)	10(20)	22	+4%
(iv)	Contraceptive condoms*	14(28)	4(8)	18	+20%
	Total usage	**42(84)**	**24(48)**	**66 (132)**	**+36%**
	None	8(16)	26(52)	34 (68)	
	Total	**50 (100)**	**50 (100)**	**100 (200)**	

Figures in parenthesis show percentages to their respective totals.

private doctor, 20 per cent went to local healer (*vaidya)* and 20 per cent went for treatment at home with indigenous concoctions.

Thus, MGNREGA has positive impact on access to health services as participant Taungya go to private doctors and *vaidyas* due to greater physical movement owing to MGNREGA participation.This was due to greater disposable income at hand and greater mobility to the urban centres owing to work sites.The reason cited by most of them is due to a regular visits of ANM/nurse to the Taungya villages from the PHC who makes the allopathic medicines available to them. Apart from that the Taungyas are historically an immigrant community of Bengal so their faith in the *Bengali local Vaids* is immense.

Place of Delivery and Assistance of Pregnant Women in Taungya

The data from Table 4.4 reveals that 70 per cent of the deliveries of pregnant Taungya women took place at home, eleven per cent with the help of relatives, seven per cent with the help of trained attendants (*dais*) and only eight per cent deliveries took place at the hospitals.

There is a difference of 12 per cent high in institutional deliveries among the participant Taungya households and 18 per cent more of pregnant females from participant Taungya household, were assisted by a nurse or a midwife during delivery. This shows that MGNREGA has positive impact on maternal health of participant Taungya households.

However, field observations showed that this percentage of institutional deliveries is of the females who are in critical situation and who have easy accessibility to the medical system due to their own parents staying near to the urban centres. Most of these women said that they stayed at their parents place till the delivery and also after that if the doctors suggested. But for the women who had no relatives in the urban centres, it was difficult to commute to the nearest urban centre for their deliveries.

Antenatal and Post Natal Care

The data in Table 4.4 reveals that only 60 per cent of total pregnant Taungya women opted for IFA tablets and TT immunisation, 20 per cent went for antenatal check ups and only 20 per cent went for post natal check ups.

There is a difference of 20 per cent high in immunisation of pregnant women of participant Taungya households. This shows that MGNREGA has positive impact on maternal health of participant Taungya households.

Field observations showed that the reason for this level of immunisation in the participantTaungya village is due to an ANM visitingTaungya village for immunisation once a month and greater physical mobility of participant Taungya women.

The Immunisation Status

Data on 0-5 years children residing in the Taungya villages in Table 4.4 reveals that out of the total sample of 60 Taungya children in the age group of 0-5 years, 52 per cent of male child and 6 per cent of female child have been immunised against vaccine preventable diseases.

Field observations showed that because of low accessibility of the villages to the township, a colossal percentage of Taungya are poor so they cannot afford costly immunisation services provided in the private nursing homes and hospitals. Although an ANM visits the villages once a month for the immunisation of pregnant women and children, they opined that during day time Taungya women having children in the age- group 0-5 year goes to field for daily labour activities leaving their children with their grand parents or elderly children, who are reluctant to vaccinate children in the absence of their parents. These reasons are responsible for lower vaccination status of children. Among the older generation of Taungya, grandparents are more biased in favour of male child than female child. Further, the vaccination status of ante-natal women is comparatively higher than the children because the procedure of vaccination cycle among children is more lengthy than that of ante-natal women.

Family Planning Status

Analysis of the Table above shows that out of 66 total sample of eligible Taungya couples in the reproductive age-group,only 14 per cent went for sterilisation, 12 per cent went for IUCD, 22 per cent opt for oral pills and 18 per cent went for contraceptive condoms. Data shows that 48 per cent users of the family planning devices were the women who have easy communication and accessibility to family planning method due to an ANM visiting their village once a month.

In terms of family planning, 48 percentage of non-participant Taungya were using family planning method and 84 per cent of participants Taungya were using family planning method. It was found that the percentage usage of family planning methods by Taungya participating in MGNREGA was 36 per cent higher than those who were not participating. This shows that MGNREGA has produced positive impact on use of family planning method among Taungya households due of greater awareness and exposure to urban centres.

Field observations showed that majority of the decisions regarding family planning were taken by the Taungya females. The awareness levels among the Taungya females was more due to their greater levels of interaction with the urban populace owing to workforce participation. More so, the counselling provided by the ANMs visiting the settled villages also helps in enhancing the awareness levels of Taungya females and in taking up any decision regarding family planning.

Table 4.5: Diseases among Taungya Household

S.No	*Area*	*Total*	*Non-participant*	*Participant*
Non Communicable Disease				
1.	Paralysis	2	2(4)	-
2.	Heart attack	4	2(4)	2(4)
3.	Blood pressure and Diabetes	14	12 (24)	2(4)
4.	Asthma	30	20 (40)	10(20)
	None		14	14
	Total	**50**	**36**	**14**
Communicable Disease				
1.	Diarrhoea	8	2 (4)	6 (12)
2.	TB	26	6 (12)	20 (40)
3.	Typhoid fever	6	-	6 (12)
4.	E-coli	10	6 (12)	4(8)
	Total	**50**	**14**	**36**
	Total	**100**	**50**	**50**

Figures in parenthesis show percentages to their respective totals.

Diseases in Taungya

The data on diseases in Table below reveal that 30 per cent of Taungya suffered from Asthma and 14 per cent from Blood pressure and Diabetes, 4 per cent from Heart attack and 2 per cent from Paralysis. However, the majority of the Taungya male and female suffered from communicable diseases. Almost 26 per cent suffer from TB and 8 per cent from water borne diseases like Diarrhoea and Typhoid fever (6 per cent) while 10 per cent from E. Coli and 8 per cent from Malaria.

Field observations showed that among the Taungyas, it was observed that as the water table lowered beyond the reach of the people, the water drawn from the well became cloudy and muddy. The Taungyas themselves described that the water shortages is not just one issue but as the whole Taungya village shares a single well as their main water source, water related diseases have increased which has effected their health. This was confirmed in the Taungya villages just by observing how the villagers use different contaminated containers from different households in pulling water out from the wells rather than just allocate one or a few containers for pulling water out from the well and pour it in everyone's container to be carried home.

Urban Contact

As enumerated in the Table above, 86 per cent Taungyas participants in MGNREGA maintained the urban contacts on weekly basis for purchasing the household essentials and 14 per cent on a daily basis to work as daily wager.

As shown in the Table above, 30 per cent of non-participant Taungya made weekly urban contacts to sell the ropes made from *Bhabar* grass and 70 per cent went to the urban areas on a daily basis for participation in labour works on a daily basis.

Field observations showed that the greater mobility and greater degree of urban contacts have led to high awareness levels of Taungyas and had adapted them to take up any kind of workforce activity.

Occupational Pattern

Data in Table above shows that 14 per cent of participants Taungya were involved in MGNREGA works and livestock while 86 per cent were involved in MGNREGA works and forest works. It was Taungya women who constituted the major MGNREGA workforce while their husband migrated to neighbouring townships for agricultural labour works. This doubled the income of the participant Taungya households. On the other hand, 48 per cent of nonparticipants Taungya men were still in the daily wages while 40 per cent were engaged in daily wage and rope making (*Baanmaking*).

Box 4.1: Field Note

Wage employment opportunity leading to self employment strategy

Shanti Devi, 52 years, living in *kaluwala* Taungya worked under MGNREGA for one year and the income that she got from MGNREGA works was used by her in starting a grocery shop. Her house was located on the road side and her health did not allow her to go for out for the labour works. Since she was the only working member of her household, she needed to work despite her ill health. When MGNREGA works were started in her village, she joined the works and accumulated her total income in her bank account for an year. After getting a lumpsum of ₹ 10,000, she invested the money in starting a grocery shop in the room of her house which faced the road. Today she earns staying within her house and can take intermittent rests for her proper health.

Source : Personal Communication.

*Fig. 4.1: Ropes (***Baan-making***) prepared from* **Bhabar** *grass.*

MGNREGA has positively impacted the occupation pattern of participant Taungya and have served the MGNREGA objective of more than 33 per cent job reservation for women in MGNREGA.

Economic Impact of Mgnrega on Taungya Community

Status of Income

As enumerated in the Table below. the income of the participant Taungya show an increase of a mean income ₹10,625 due to participation in MGNREGA and afforestation works. The paired t test show a significant difference in the income levels before and after MGNREGA participation.Here the income levels of the participant Taungya household has increased due to participation of Taungya women in MGNREGA and their husband as daily wages labourer in the household.

Table 4.6: Income Levels of Participant Taungya

Category	*Participants*	
	Before	*After*
Mean	47,978	58,603
S.D	8,940	22,826
t test (paired-t)	4.482*	

*significant at 5%

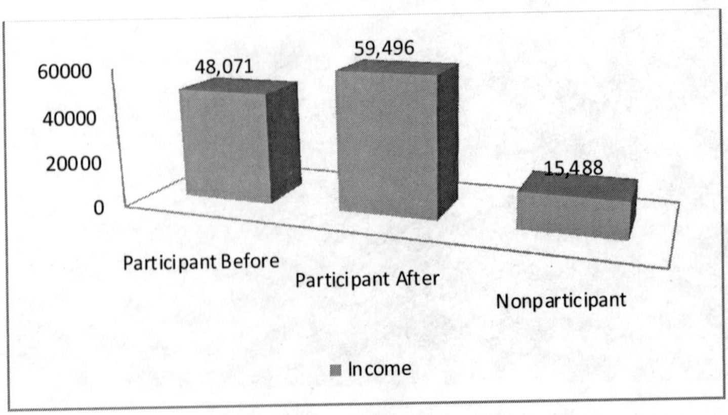

Fig. 4.2: Income levels of Participant and Non-participant Taungyas.

Table 4.7: Impact of MGNREGA on Income of the Taungya Participants

Particulars	*Annual Income*			
	Off farm	*On farm*	*MGNREGA*	*Total*
Before MGNREGA	43,565	4,413	-	47,978
	(90.8%)	(7.5%)		
After MGNREGA	43,267 (72.72%)	6,336 (10.64%)	9000 (15.12%)	58,603
Net change	-298	+1923	9000	+10,625
t value (paired–t)	**4.48***			

*significant at 5 per cent

The annual income of the Taungya participants from different sources is given in Table 4.7. Before working under MGNREGA, the annual income of the participants from Off farm activities and On farm activities was of ₹ 43,658 and ₹ 4,413 respectively, which added to ₹ 47,978. After working under MGNREGA programme, the income earned from Off farm activities was ₹ 43,267 and On farm activities was ₹ 6,336. The MGNREGA wages added to it a total of ₹ 58,603 showing a net change of ₹ 10,625 to the total annual income. In total income, the share of Off farm income was highest (72.7 per cent), followed by income from MGNREGA (15.1 per cent) and then income from On farm activities (10.6 per cent).The paired t test showed a significant difference at 5 per cent level of significance in the income of participant Taungya before and after MGNREGA. The null hypothesis of Participation in MGNREGA has no impact on the income levels of Taungya is rejected and MGNREGA has produced a significant impact on the income levels of participant Taungya.

The income earned from daily wages after being employed under MGNREGA programme is due to the regular employment in the afforestation works and other works carried out by the Forest Department when MGNREGA works are not going on. Taungya community has been in the afforestation works since the British times and this is one knowledge that they were experts so MGNREGA brought to their doorstep the kind of work which was skill specific to them.

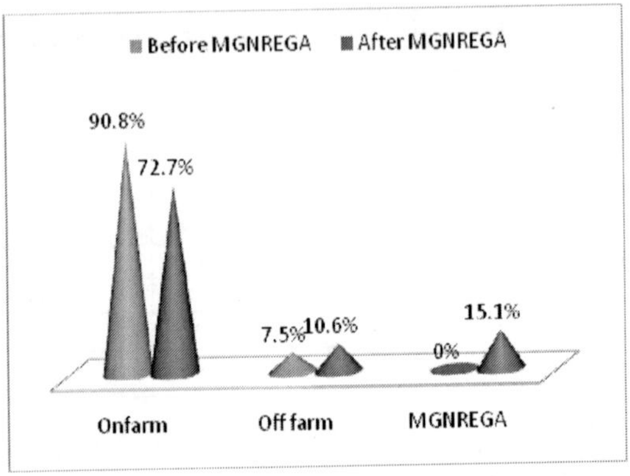

Fig. 4.3: Impact of MGNREGA on Income of the Taungya beneficiaries.

Box 4.2: Field Note

MGNREGA helped in strengthening the wage negotiation capacity

Reshamlal, a 65 year old illiterate native of Bhagwatpur. He lives with his wife and one son. He has a daughter, who got married five years back, and currently lives with her husband. He is landless and works as a daily wage labourer. Reshamlal works in MGNREGA and when his hundred days of work with MGNREGA is over, he works for the landlords or other private work. Five years back, Reshamlal was working with landlords on a yearly basis. He discontinued this as he felt that the work was very hard and the wage was very meagre. He says, that working with the landlords is like an obligation; further he added that when he was working with the landlords, he was socially excluded as he could not attend any kind of social events like marriages or lunches offered by relatives on various occasions. If he took a day off, his landlord would cut wages for almost 2 days. He said that many labourers, who were previously working with the landlords on a yearly basis, are now working in the MGNREGA. Their first preference is to work in the MGNREGA and then only they are willing to work for the landlords but only on the daily basis. They sell their services to the highest bidder charging higher daily wage rate due to MGNREGA. Reshamlal says that five years back, he used to get ₹ 25 as daily wages but now there is drastic change in the daily wage rate. Even a farmer now pays ₹ 60 –70 per day. The reason is the increase in the daily wages because of the MGNREGA. He feels that in the absence of MGNREGA the labourers had no other choice than to work for the farmers at a daily wage of ₹ 25. Reshamlal got a small plot from the Gram Panchayat to build a house. He has built a *kaccha house* for himself using the money saved from the annual payment received from landlords. 3 months ago, Reshamlal replaced the tiles (*Chhapar*) with the money he earned from MGNREGA. Reshamlal says that as compared to the work in MGNREGA, working for the landlords meant hard work and extended hours. When working as group in MGNREGA, they could chat and discuss various topics which made it a very enjoyable experience.

Source: Personal Communication.

Expenditure Pattern

As depicted in Table below, the mean expenditure of the participant Taungya household before MGNREGA was ₹ 1,02,836 and after MGNREGA was ₹ 1,35,173. There was a significant difference in the mean expenditure with a net change of ₹ 32,337. The results of Paired t test showed a significant difference between expenditure of the participant Taungya before and after MGNREGA. The percentage change in the expenditure before and after MGNREGA of participant Gujjar have increased by 30.69 per cent. Enhanced incomes through MGNREGA have helped in diversification of expenditure and enlargement of the consumption basket of participant Taungya household. Thus, participation in MGNREGA had a significant and positive impact on consumption expenditure of Taungya household.

Table 4.8: Impact of MGNREGA on Expenditure and Credits of the Participants.

Particulars	*Annual Expenditure*	*Annual Credit*
Before MGNREGA	1,02,836	54,765
After MGNREGA	1,35,173	75,677
Absolute change	32,337	20,912
Percent change	30.69	38.18
t value (paired–t)	12.262*	6.16*

*significant at 5%

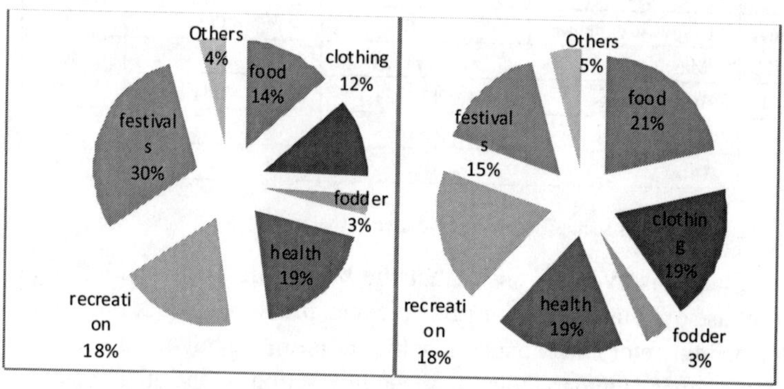

Non Participant Taungya *Participant Taungya*

Fig. 4.4: Consumption Pattern of Participant and Nonparticipant Taungya.

Credit Facilities

As the Table above shows that the mean amount of loan taken by participant Taungya is around ₹ 54,765 and after the advent of MGNREGA the amount got increased to ₹ 75,677. The paired t test values showed a significant difference in the amount of credit participant Taungya took before and after participation in MGNREGA.

The increase in the credit system is due to an enhanced standard of living as gets evident from the consumption pattern. Participant Taungyas spend more money on food and clothing than prior to participation. This shows that MGNREGA has increased their purchasing power and has also led to their access to formal and nonformal credit networks.

Reason of Credit

As shown in Table 4.9, after participation in MGNREGA, 72 per cent of participant Taungya took loans for marriage expenses, 22 per cent on buying of assets and 6 per cent on other item of utility. Among the Non-participant Taungya, 72 per cent took loan to meet their daily domestic expenses, 14 per cent for other expenses and 14 per cent for buying assets.

Table 4.9: Reason of Credit of Taungya

		Participants	*Non-Participants*	*Total*
(ii)	Domestic expenses	0	36 (72)	36
(iv)	Marriage	36 (72)	0	36
(v)	Buying assets	11 (22)	7 (14)	18
(vi)	Others	3 (6)	7 (14)	10
	Total	**50**	**50**	**100**

Figures in parenthesis show percentages to their respective totals.

Field observations show that the buying of the assets entailed purchase of household things like bicycle, pressure cooker, fan, trunk and bedding etc. The expansion in the choice of the buying of material possession is owing to their enhanced interactions in the urban centres and also due to the greater mobility of womenfolk. However, it was observed that their reasons for credit dependence takes a different shift after participation in MGNREGA. Since after participation in

MGNREGA, most of their domestic needs and food security needs are being met with the wages of MGNREGA works. The higher end needs like expenses entailed in marriage and in terms of some health crisis are met with loans.

This data makes it evident that Taungyas have an aptitude towards a higher standard of living and believe in improving their living conditions. This desire has increased their dependence on the credit facilities resulting in higher amounts of debt.

Chapter - 5

Wage Employment and Women Empowerment

Empowerment is a process of social and economic building leading to greater social participation, to greater decision-making and economic control along with enhanced mobility among women of Gujjar and Taungya community. Empowerment is the expansion of assets and capabilities of poor people to participate in, negotiate with, influence, control and hold accountable institutions that affect their lives (Deepa Narayan, 2006). Empowerment needs to move beyond a socio-economic institutional perspective which assumes that individual socio-economic characteristics such as women's education, labour force participation and income and access to resources will determine a woman's ability to exercise control over forces of adversity, improving her power relations with men. Indeed empirical evidence shows that despite improvements in education, income and access to resources and credit in the last 10-15 years, women's position in the areas of health, decision-making, employment and freedom of rights have not improved significantly as indicated by human and development indicators (Pradhan, 2003). Empowerment is the process by which the powerless gain greater control over the circumstances of their lives. It includes both control over resources (physical, human, intellectual, financial) and ideology (beliefs, values, attitudes). It means greater self-confidence, and an inner transformation of one's consciousness that enables one to overcome external barriers to accessing resources or changing traditional ideologies.

This chapter aims at measuring the empowerment levels of women of the respective community after the advent of MGNREGA in their villages. A Principal Component Analysis was conducted on the data collected on selected 23 variables and from 140 respondents (70 women Taungya community). From the PCA, pertinent factors were deduced that contribute to the empowerment of women in Taungya community. An index on women empowerment was prepared from the deduced factors and a qualitative analysis based on the frequency and percentage quantification was done of each factor. A paired t test was applied on the empowerment scores of before and after MGNREGA participation in order to validate the hypothesis.

Social and Economic Empowerment of Taungya Women

After the PCA, 2 factors with 10 variables were deduced that contribute to the empowerment of women in Taungya community. The factors deduced were named as: factor 1-Decision-making in social matters, financial matters and physical mobility. The factor 2- was named as Work participation, Ownership of livestock and other household assets, Decision-making in family planning, access to credit and Social participation as given in the Table 5.1. The value of Cronbach's Alpha reliability Coefficient for both the factors was .979 (factor 1) and .877 (factor 2). Since value of Cronbach's alpha reliability Coefficient for both the factors was more than .7 so both the factors are contributing to the women empowerment of Taungya women. An index on women empowerment was prepared from the deduced factors. The indices scores of the deduced factors in the order of their relevance has been given in the Table 5.1:

The data in Table 5.1 demonstrates that the factor contributing maximum to the empowerment of Taungya women is Decision-making in physical mobility as they have a relatively better autonomy of free movement. Taungya communities follow Hindu religion which does not culturally restrict their mobility. It is a general rule that the Taungya women have a lot of say in the matters related to social matters especially in regards to the education and marriage of children. The Taungya women are free to seek formal employment opportunities and are socially allowed to intermingle and work with the male folk. The other indicators of empowerment for Taungya women are ownership of other asset, control own income and control natural resource base showing the medium hold of Taungya women on the household and her surroundings. The variable falling lowest in the

Empowerment Index is social participation thus, reflecting their subjugation owing to the male dominance in the community eventually, the women stay out of the community decision-making processes through informal institutions like Van Panchayats.

Table 5.1: Factors contributing to Empowerment of Women among Taungya community (Rotated Component Matrix of Taungya women)

	Components	
	1	***2***
Social Participation		**.731**
Decision-making in Social Matters	.933	
Decision-making in Financial Matters	.956	
Decision-making in Physical Mobility	**.968**	
Workforce Participation		-.791
Livestock Ownership		.899
Owner Other Assets		.987
Control Own Income		.986
Control Family Planning		.986
Access to Credit		.884

Extraction Method: Principal Component Analysis. Rotation Method: Varimax with Kaiser Normalisation.

Major Factors Contributing to Women Empowerment in Taungya Women

The factor contributing maximum to the empowerment of Taungya women is Decision-making in physical mobility as they have a relatively better autonomy of free movement. Taungya communities follow Hindu religion which does not culturally restrict their mobility. It is a general rule that the Taungya women have a lot of say in the matters related to social matters especially in regards to the education and marriage of children. The Taungya women are free to seek formal employment opportunities and are socially allowed to intermingle and work with the male folk. The other indicators of empowerment for Taungya women are ownership of other asset, control own income and control natural resource base showing the medium hold of Taungya women on the household and her surroundings.

Table 5.2: Decision-making in Social, Financial and Physical Mobility in Taungya women

	Variables	*Frequency*	*Percentage*
(i)	**Decision-making in Physical Mobility**		
	Along with someone else	10	14.3
	Along with husband	7	10
	Alone	53	75.7
(ii)	**Decision-making in Social Matters**		
	Not at all	20	28.5
	Along with husband	3	4.2
	Alone	47	67.1
(iii)	**Decision-making in Financial Matter**		
	Along with someone else	3	4.2
	Along with husband	18	25.7

(i) Decision-making in Physical Mobility

As shown in Table 5.2, among the Taungya women, 75.7 per cent of women moved out alone while 24.3 per cent of women moved out along with someone else.

Women in Taungya social and religious standing gives them the autonomy of free movement with no restrictions. As Taungya is a Hindu scheduled castes (belonging to *Chamar community*) so culturally women are allowed for a free intermingling of genders. Women in Taungya are free to visit their work sites, healthcare facilities, relatives and market areas around the urban areas which are at least 10-15 kms away from their settlements. Taungya women travel to their worksite which is normally at the periphery of the forests where they need to travel on foot for at least 1-2 kms or by bus too. It is the Taungya women who normally carry an ailing child to the *Local vaidya* or a private doctor as the man of the family are involved in the labour works at distant township. Any kind of medical emergency is dealt by the Taungya females as they cannot afford to wait for their husbands to come back as they reach late in the night and are normally drunk. As their villages are settled villages on the periphery of forests, there is no provision of transportation reaching their villages so they have to walk on foot for at least 3-4 kms in order to reach their villages once they get down from the local transport connecting them to the urban centres. Taungya women normally form a group to visit the local *haats* and *melas* that are held on the festivals around their villages. The Taungya women who are not into the formal employment look after the livestock which is normally small ruminants. It is the women-folk who take them to the forests and the areas adjoining the forest for grazing purpose. Taungya women visit their relatives as and when required and she does not seek out for the permission of her husband or in-laws in doing so.

A young married women told that earlier young women going to do labour works was looked down upon but in MGNREGA, since the work is at the sites within the close proximity of their own villages, man folk have turned more confident of sending us for work outside the houses. Women feel more secure and have money along with being financially independent.

Box 5.1: Field Note

Taungya women go an extra mile alone for family need

Beena Devi, 51 years old lady is involved in afforestation activity of the Forest Department. Her only daughter is detected with a cancerous lump near her neck portion. For the diagnosis of this lump, it was Beena who accompanied her daughter to the nearest big town *Saharanpur* which is 40 kms away from their village. She took her daughter to the government hospital and stayed there for weeks together along with her daughter alone till the final diagnosis was completed. As the cancer was at the advanced level, Beena was recommended to leave for Mumbai for the final treatment. Upon my interaction with her, she sounded most determined to take her daughter to Mumbai and was saving every penny out of her hardwork for her daughters' treatment.

Source: Personal Communication.

(ii) Decision-making in Social Matters

As shown in Table 5.2, among the Taungya women, 68 per cent of women took the decisions alone while 27.1 per cent of them did not take the decisions at all and 4.3 per cent of them made the decisions along with their husband.

It is the Taungya women who take major decisions regarding the education and marriage of their sons and daughters. The general observation is that although they have meagre say in the community related matters but when it comes to the matters of the family life, it is the Taungya women who lead by example. It is an unsaid rule in a Taungya household that it is the women who manage the matters pertaining to children and also the social networking of the family within the community. Any household visited on fieldwork depicted a very harmonious relationship between the mother-in-law and daughter-in-laws. In Taungya community, girls and boys are married at a young age so most of the daughter-in-laws were young girls who were treated like daughters in their in-laws house. The duty of a daughter-in-law was to just attend to the daily household chores. She was not allowed to join any formal work employment opportunity rather the mother-in-law would go for the work. The young daughter-in-law tends to small ruminants at home but never takes them out for grazing. It was amazing that despite being a female researcher; still young daughter-in-laws always offered water with a veil on their face. The reason sensed was owing to the male escorts with me. Mostly, it is the mother who emphasised on the education of both daughters and sons at the school within the village. As Taungya is a settled village so as part of the settlement plan of their village, they were given a primary school within 1 km of proximity. The results of the Taungya women passion towards education gets evident when our data showed almost 90 per cent of educated youth.

Box 5.2: Field Note

Education prime for Taungya Women

Shanto Devi, 55 years of the Kaluwala Taungya village has taken up the mission of educating the young girls of the community. As the settled Kaluwala village is almost at the proximity of the forest and it is an elephant corridor. The road to the school is a narrow pavement in the forest area covered with Taungya plantations on both side of the village making it more dangerous for the young girls to travel alone to the school. It is Shanto Devi who accompanies the girls group to the school and sits there outside till the school finishes. She then accompanies the girls back to the village. Upon interaction, she told that it is the most satisfying experience of her life. She says, "I always wanted to study but could not study so I feel I am living my dream of getting education through these girls. I feel complete.

Source: Personal Communication.

(iii) Decision-making in Financial Matter

As shown in Table 5.2, among the Taungya women, 70 per cent of women took the decisions alone while 25.7 per cent of women did not take any decisions and 4.2 per cent of the women made financial decisions along with someone else.

In the Taungya community, it is the woman who takes care of the major household expenditure so she is the one to manage the finances. Taungya women are active in contributing to the family income as their formal workforce participation is high. Taungya women manage the finances of the household by having saving accounts in the Post Office. Although the Post Office is normally 10 kms away from their settlements but owing to their free movement, Taungya women always find time to go to the Post Office once a month atleast to deposit in their savings account. Most of the women shared a unanimous viewpoint that with their kind of lifestyle, if they donot take up the pains of going to the Post Office to deposit their savings, the whole money gets wasted in merriment.

The Taungya villages shows the extent to which MGNREGA has been gender friendly and have raised their economic access along with dignity and esteem. This economic independence has also led to changing of gender equations and relations within the family institutions. Taungya women reported that, "My husband helps me in the household chores once I come back from work site and he looks after the children when I go for working in MGNREGA."

The women opined that today they are in a better position to take decisions regarding their children's health and education as they also contribute to the household income. Their husband has begun to value their advises and suggestions and mostly decisions are based on consensual understanding. However, it was reported in the FGDs that it was their husbands who operated their passbooks. There is a need to change the perception that "we will get work when the Forest Department starts the afforestation drives." Since these villages are on the periphery of the forests, it is the Forest Department who assigns them MGNREGA works under the afforestation drives.

Box 5.3: Field Note

An entrepreneur in Taungya women

Geeta, an aged lady with her husband expired for last 8 years, worked as labourer in agricultural land after walking for odd 10 kms so at times, she worked for just 10-15 days in a month and used that money for the rest of the month. More so, there was no work assurance upon reaching work sites.

But just 3 years back in 2008 when MGNREGA came to the Forest Department, she worked in it and earned Rs 8000 after working for 80 days. She invested that money in starting a grocery shop as her house was on road and feels happy with the effort, "This money came at a time when I needed it the most. This scheme is a hope for people like me who stay away from the work areas and at least we know that we will get the work once we reach the worksite." The shop happens to be her main source of livelihood now and she does not need to work under any employment now.

Source: Personal Communication.

Factors contributing least to Women Empowerment in Taungya women

The variable falling lowest in the Empowerment Index is social participation thus, reflecting their subjugation owing to the male dominance in the community eventually, the women stay out of the community decision-making processes through informal institutions like Van Panchayats.

(iv) Work Participation

The data showed in Table 5.3 that the participation of women is 93 per cent in the formal occupation. Almost in all the Taungya villages, most of the women were involved in MGNREGA activities being run by the Forest Department. The rest seven per cent of women are involved in livestock rearing and *Baan-making*. Apart from the MGNREGA works, women are involved in the afforestation works undertaken by the Forest Department for the rest of the year. The reason cited by forest officials is that Taungya women are hardworking and quite acquainted with the afforestation activity due to knowledge about traditional Taungya system of cultivation. Forest Officials

Table 5.3: Work participation, Ownership of livestock and other household assets, Decision-making in family planning, access to credit and Social participation

	Variables	*Frequency*	*Percentage*
iv.	**Work Participation**		
	Not working presently	4	7.1
	Working in family occupation	28	38.6
	Working in formal Occupation	38	54.3
v.	**Ownership of Other Assets**		
	Not at all	22	31.4
	Joint ownership	18	25.7
	Alone	30	42.9
vi.	**Control own Income**		
	Not at all	22	31.4
	Along with husband	19	27.2
	Alone	29	41.4
vii.	**Ownership of Livestock**		
	Not at all	38	54.3
	Joint Ownership	2	1.4
	Alone	30	44.3
viii.	**Access to Credit**		
	Credit through family	39	55.9
	Husband	3	4.3
	Self	28	40
ix.	**Decision Making in Family Planning**		
	Not at all	22	31.4
	Along with husband	19	27.1
	Alone	29	41.4
x.	**Social Participation**		
	No participation	39	55.7
	Participation in formal organisation	9	31.4
	Participation in informal organisation	22	12.9

emphasised that more women were required in afforestation activities as plantation of a seedling required a ratio of 1:2 of man and woman ratio. Under the Taungya system the whole family planted trees in the fixed nurseries allotted to them and took care of the allotted land and trees under it for the next five years. Taungya women have mastered this skill of plantation early from their childhood days. However, it was the middle aged and older women who were involved in this work participation and most of the younger females were involved into livestock rearing and *baan-making* which required them to stay at home. Taungya women are experts in *baan-making* and in the process of *baan-making*, men just have the role of procuring the *Bhabar* grass as a raw product and then they go to the urban weekly market for selling of the *baan* prepared by women. Women are involved at every stage of production of *baan* from beating of grasses to crushing, thrashing, drying and weaving of the rope. Every stage of *baan-making* demands a lot of physical labour and Taungya women are strong enough to stand to all of it to make extra earnings to support the family.

***Fig. 5.1: Taungya women involved in* Baan-making.**

The settled Taungya village of Bhagwatpur stands as an example of exceptional women participation in the activities of MGNREGA. Data showed 90 per cent of the participation is of the women in the MGNREGA as the works are carried out by the Forest Department. Since women earlier to the advent of MGNREGA were involved in the afforestation drive run by the forest division, they share a good reputation of hardworking and disciplined workers. Forest officials prefer women over the Taungya men due to their sincerity and commitment. A young married woman commented, "Since us all women from the same village work in MGNREGA, we feel secure coming together and going back to work in forests together."

Since Taungya women have been involved in the Taungya system of cultivation so they are quite experts in the management of natural resources. This being the sole reason for their involvement in the afforestation activities of the Forest Department. Taungya women are also experts in the farming of different cropping patterns along with the afforestation activities. They have knowledge of which herb and shrub grows better under the shades of the trees leading to the maximisation of the land patterns. One thing that gets evident is that women tend to know more about the medicinal value of plants since they are the ones who indulge more in the forest peripheral areas. Again it is the young Taungya females who take their livestock for grazing so they are more aware of the 'good' and 'bad' areas around the place. They know precisely which are the forbidden areas in order to avoid the attack from wild animals like *neel gai,* wild elephants etc.

(v) Ownership of Other Assets

As shown in Table 5.3, among the Taungya women, 42.9 per cent owned the sole possession of assets, 31.4 per cent did not own any assets while 25.7 per cent owned a joint possession of ownership.

Fig. 5.2: A Taungya village.

Fig. 5.3: Taungya hut tenement.

Taungya women seem to have an ownership of other assets like jewellery and household items. Since Taungya women have total control on their incomes and they have the discretion of utilising their income. A Taungya household is a mix of rural and urban style of living with a greater interest in everything that is flashy. The women use more kerosene stoves and also every household had a flashy rope woven bed (*chorpoy*). Taungya women weave these beds themselves. Every Taungya hut has a distinct corner for every utility in the form of kitchen, bathroom and bedroom along with grain storage room. Taungya women seem to decorate their houses by drawing beautiful flowers and leaves. The distinct feature of a Taungya household is the *verandah* which holds water pots of clay for the storage of water and any and every passerby can drink from those pots. Every Taungya hut has an extension of another straw hut tenement which acts like a storeroom of a big steel trunk and a *chorpoy*.

(vi) Control Own Income

As shown in Table 5.3, among the Taungya women, 41.4 per cent of women had control over their own income, 31.4 per cent of them did not control their income at all and 27.2 per cent of women controlled their own income along with their husband.

Taungya women have a mixed approach of handling their own income. The younger females who are participating tend to hand over their incomes to their in-laws and husband. Most of the women decide along with their husband the area in which they need to spend their money. It is mainly in the education and meeting of the social exchanges that women use their money. Most of the time, it is the women who makes arrangements for a marriage ceremony of her children or in that case, she is around for attending to any medical emergency so she utilises her money in these areas more. There seems to be no questioning of however, she uses her money. At times on the field, young females in FGDs shared that they were allowed to keep a part of their incomes by their in-laws which they spend in buying decorative jewellery and fashionable items from weekly *haats*. Weekly *haats* are taken as an occasion of merriment where women enjoy whatever income is left after utilisation from their household needs. However, women control their income more in terms of productive areas than the merriment aspect.

Box 5.4: Field Note

Taungya women right to quality life through MGNREGA

Shanti, 35 years old women have been working in the scheme since its inception in 2008. She looked happy earning ₹ 9000 for 90 days. She has spent her earnings on consumer items, food and also on healthcare and children's education. She says, "I feel the freedom of choice. I can buy things that appeal to me like bangles and toys for the children."

Source: Personal Communication.

(vii) Ownership of Livestock

As shown in Table 5.3, among the Taungya women, 54.3 per cent of women did not own any livestock, 44.3 per cent of women own the livestock and only 1.4 per cent shared a joint ownership of livestock. Taungya women dwell on what they earn and do not get any financial support from the husband or her natal family. They do not have any livestock under her name although they tend to them but the control is totally of husband and in-laws over the livestock. This is based on the fact that no Taungya women gets livestock as a part of Hindu inheritance laws and no livestock as part of her dowry so the livestock is solely the property of the husband to own and control.

Box 5.5: Field Notes

Taungya women building asset through MGNREGA

Seema, a young married female who worked in MGNREGA last year says, "The gap between the work and wage payment is so high that we tend to forget the number of days we worked on a site." She lives with her husband and children and is quite keen to work all 100 days. She emphasises, "Working in MGNREGA has granted me monetary security to spend more money on children's education, household items, food and for treatment of my children if they fall sick. I have added value to my assets by buying three goats as my husband sells milk too." Her husband sells the milk to supplement their income. With regular earnings from MGNREGA now, they are able to concentrate more to optimise returns from milk sale. "It is my husband who takes majority of the decisions but I have begun to have some say in expenditure especially if it is about my earning. I invested my earnings in increasing the livestock and in increasing the income flow in the family." She smiles and adds, "Now I am a proud owner of three goats." She shares further that most of the woman working in MGNREGA have a bank account in their names but they spend a lot of money in going to bank every time and checking it if in case the money is in account or not.

Source: Personal Communication.

One interesting fact that comes out of the data is that the oldest women of the family has the eventual control on the livestock and it is she who takes the eventual decision pertaining to buying and selling of livestock. Taungya people have no special connection with their livestock unlike Gujjar people. Taungya generally see livestock as instant cash available at hand in terms of crisis. Most of the younger Taungya females grudged on the presence of small ruminants which only added o their household chores and left them with little time for themselves. Henceforth, ownership of livestock is never taken as a symbol of power but merely as a necessity by Taungyas.

(viii) Access to Credit

As shown in Table 5.3, among Taungya women, 55.9 per cent of women got credit through the family while 40 per cent of them had access to credit through self and only four per cent got the credit through their husband.

In the Taungya community, women have access to both formal and informal credit networks. Mostly older women of the family are into the workforce participation and own their own savings accounts in bank which makes them eligible for the loans in case of emergency. Also the women in Taungya community share good working rapport with the forest officials and due to their recommendations; they get easy loans from the local *baniyas* of the area. In order to meet an instant need of the family like in any health diseases, it is the Taungya women who get the loan from the local village petty shopkeepers and this trust is based on the fact that these shopkeepers know that this female will repay back their loans by working extra hard. Here a point that gets highlighted is the low social credibility of Taungya male that are into drinking and making merriment.

MGNREGA has given them 'immediate income opportunity and seems to be changing the social fabric of the society. Rani Devi says, "MGNREGA money has helped us in increasing our savings habit and it provides us with a financial security in lean periods. Earlier in labour works, we got wages on daily basis so there were no savings as the liquid income was used instantly in family expenditure." The villagers agreed that their savings in bank account has got them out of the clutches of moneylenders who gave them loans at higher rate of interests and at times, in cases of non-payment, they had to part ways with their livestock. So MGNREGA has on one hand enhanced their purchasing power and savings but has reduced their credit loans.

(ix) Decision-making in Family Planning

As shown in Table 5.3, among Taungya women, 41.4 per cent of women had total control over family income; 31.4 per cent of women did not have any control over the family income while 27.1 per cent of women controlled the family income along with their husband.

Field observations showed that majority of the decisions regarding family planning are taken by the Taungya females. The awareness levels among the Taungya females are more due to their greater levels of interaction with the urban populace owing to workforce participation. More so, the counselling provided by the ANMs visiting the settled villages also helps in enhancing the awareness levels of Taungya females and in taking up any decision regarding family planning.

(x) Social Participation

As shown in Table 5.3, among Taungya women, 55.7 per cent of women did not participate in any organisation, 31.4 per cent of them participated in formal organisations like Gram Panchayat and MGNREGA meetings while 12.9 per cent of women participated in informal organisation.

Taungya women although have all the autonomy of free mobility and workforce participation yet their social positioning is commanded greatly by the male counterparts of the Taungya community. Women folk are not allowed to speak in the public forum and are allowed to be the mute spectators. Although the elderly females are a part of informal community meetings which seeks to decide on some important agenda but Taungya females have developed that habit of being 'silent' in the public domain so they merely yield to all the decisions that are taken by men-folk. Due to the emergence of schemes like MGNREGA which makes it mandatory for women participation in work and their presence in the proceedings of Gram Panchayat meetings, Taungya women have got a platform to get exposed to the formal proceedings of work force. But here too they are there for the very reason of being required there. The one most subjugating aspect of the male folk over the communication of female viewpoint is controlled to the extent that in the FGDs with the females, every time a question was posed to a woman, the answer came out of a male.

E.g. a Female in one of the FGD emphasised that women under MGNREGA were being paid ₹ 80 against ₹ 120 paid to a male. She was instantly shrugged and asked to keep silence by the menfolk. However, upon walking a bit of distance, the women folk followed me and validated the fact given by that female.

Although the women still showed low social participation in the Gram Panchayat meetings, they seemed quite aware of their rights in MGNREGA. However, still the social conditions do not allow them to attend the meetings.

Impact of MGNREGA on Socioeconomic Empowerment of Women in Taungya Community

As enumerated in Table below, the Women Empowerment Index shows that Taungya women before MGNREGA had least score in decision-making in financial and physical mobility along with ownership of household assets and control own income. The highest score was in Access to credit. After MGNREGA, the lowest score was in social participation and highest score in decision-making in physical mobility. The factor that had no change in score after MGNREGA is ownership of livestock. This showed that Taungya women even after earning from MGNREGA, restricted themselves from investing in livestock from the income generated. The impact was seen majorly in decision-making in physical mobility as prior to MGNREGA, Taungya women move in and around the adjoining areas without any escort be it for work or for visiting relatives but after MGNREGA, they have begun to go to distant townships for withdrawing their wages from nearest post office which is 10 kms away. The change in score was observed least in social participation as the women in Taungya community are subjugated by the men folk and not allowed to speak out in the formal or informal public forums. This shows that despite increase in physical mobility and enhanced female incomes, the social position still remains the same for Taungya women. The factor that showed negative impact was in terms of access to credit.

Table 5.4: Impact and Differences in Empowerment Before and After MGNREGA in Taungya Women

Independent Variable	***Empowerment Index Score***			***chi square Results***		
	Before MGNREGA	***After MGNREGA***	***Difference***	χ^2	***df***	***Asymp sig (2sided)***
Work Participation	1.45	2.38	0.93	Dependent variable		
Social Participation	1.62	**1.75**	0.13	47.01	4	.000**
Decision-making in Family Planning	1.82	2.35	0.53	28.42	4	.000**
Decision-making in Social Matters	1.84	**2.44**	0.6	45.75	4	.000**
Decision-making in Financial matter	**1.32**	2.44	**1.12**	48.84	4	.000**
Decision-making in Physical Mobility	**1.32**	**2.75**	**1.43**	59.65	2	.000**
Ownership of Livestock	**1.9**	1.9	**0**	24.11	4	.000**
Ownership of Other Assets	1.32	2.11	0.79	63.57	4	.000**
Control own Income	1.32	2.11	0.79	60.49	4	.000**
Access to Credit	**2.3**	**1.84**	**-0.46**	22.28	4	.000**
Overall Index value	**0.54**	**0.73**	**0.19**			
t value (Paired)		**3.26***				

*Significant at 5%** Significant at 1%NS- Non-significant.

Furthermore, as the impact of MGNREGA is to be assessed on the empowerment levels of women so chi square test has been used to see the level of association between empowerment of women and workforce participation taken as proxy variable for MGNREGA participation.The results of the chi square is given in the Table above despite having economic independence, Taungya women have low social standing and were not allowed to voice their concerns on public platforms. Highly significant positive association at one per cent level of significance was found between respondents' workforce participation and decisions in social matters. In Taungya community, it was the working females or the older women of the household who have financial control but younger women are not involved in decision-making process. Highly significant positive association at one per cent level of significance was found between respondents' workforce participation and decisions regarding financial matters. Highly significant positive association at one per cent level of significance was found between respondents' workforce participation and ownership of other assets. Taungya women had partial or lack of total control over their income as they were young women of a joint family system who give their money to the husband or in-laws. Highly significant positive association at one per cent level of significance was found between respondents' workforce participation and control of their own incomes. Taungya women have high decision-making power with regards to fertility control and usage of family planning methods. Significant but medium positive association at one per cent level of significance was found between respondents' workforce participation and decision of using family planning methods. It was found that in Taungya community, there was no concept of ownership of livestock by Taungya women. Significant but medium positive association at one per cent level of significance was found between respondents' workforce participation and ownership of livestock. Since Taungya women were involved in formal workforce so their accessibility to formal banking system was greater and form a network with the forest officials who recommend them for loan application. Significant but medium positive association at one per cent level of significance was found between respondents' workforce participation and access to credit. It was only the older Taungya women who participate in the informal gatherings and community meetings for some collective decision to be taken. Highly significant positive association at one per cent level of significance was found between respondents' workforce participation and social participation.

The overall index value of women empowerment before MGNREGA was .54 and after MGNREGA was .73 showing an improvement by .19. The t values revealed that there was significant difference in five per cent level of significance in mean values of empowerment of Taungya women before and after taking up MGNREGA which clearly revealed the fact that income generating activities significantly contributed for enhancement in empowerment. This leads to rejection of the proposed hypothesis that there is no significant difference in the empowerment levels of women empowerment before and after MGNREGA. An alternate hypothesis that MGNREGA has significant impact on the empowerment levels of women in Taungya community was accepted.

Constraints to Empowerment in Taungya Women

The constraints in empowerment as perceived by Taungya women are furnished in Table below:

Table 5.5: Factors constraining the Empowerment in Taungya women

Reasons	*Frequency*	*Percentage*
Taungya women		
Dual responsibility of households and economic activities	4	5.6
Lack of freedom to take decisions	3	4.2
Lack of social participation due to cultural constraints	35	49.3
Doubts on women capabilities	24	33.8
Ego problems of men folk	5	7
Total	**70**	**100**

Taungya women emphasised that lack of social participation due to cultural norms (49.3 per cent) as the major constraint. The other constraints were lack of freedom to take decisions (4.2 per cent), lack of social participation due to cultural norms (49.3 per cent). The other constraints were lack of freedom to take decisions (4.2 per cent), ego problems of men folk (7 per cent), doubts on women capabilities (33.8 per cent) and they are over burdened with dual responsibility of managing households and economic activities (5.6 per cent).

Gender analysis and women empowerment through social relations approach

Gender analysis refers to the variety of methods used to understand the relationships between men and women, their access to resources, their activities, and the constraints they face relative to each other. Gender analysis offers information to understand women's and men's access to and control over resources that can be used to address disparities, challenge systemic inequalities (most often faced by women), and build efficient and equitable solutions. Gender analysis is inadvertently a part of socio-economic analysis. A complete socio-economic analysis would amount for inclusion of gender relations, as gender is a factor in all social and economic relations. An analysis of gender relations provides information on the different conditions those women and men face, and the different effects that policies and programmes may have on them because of their situations.

Such information can inform and improve policies and programmes, and is essential in ensuring that the different needs of both women and men are met.

Social Relations Approach

The ***Social Relations Approach*** is a method of analysing existing gender inequalities in the distribution of resources, responsibilities and power and for designing policies and programmes which transforms women to be agents of their own development. The framework is based on concepts rather than tools to focus on the associations between people and their relationship to resources and activities- and how these are re-worked through 'institutions' such as the state or the market.

Kabeer (1996), states that a narrow use of the Social Relations Approach, probing a particular institution, will emphasise how gender inequality is shaped and reproduced in individual institutions. A broader use, focusing on a number of institutions in a given context, will disclose how gender and other inequalities cross- cut each other through dissimilar institutions' interaction, thus producing situations of detailed disadvantage for individuals.

The framework of social relations approach comprises of the following main concepts:

(i) Development as increasing human well being;

(ii) Social relations;

(iii) Institutional analysis.

In the Social Relations Approach, development is chiefly about increasing human well-being. Human well-being is interpreted as concerning survival, security and autonomy, where autonomy means the ability to participate fully in those decisions that shape one's choices and one's life chances, at both the personal and the collective level.

As per the framework given by Kabeer, she uses the term 'social relations' to elucidate the structural associations that produce and reproduce systemic differences in the positioning of different groups of people. Such relationships decide who we are, what our roles and responsibilities are, and what claims we can make; they decide our rights, and the control that we have over own lives and those of others.

The institutional analysis looks at the fundamental causes of gender inequality are not restricted to the household and family but are reproduced across a series of institutions, including the international community, the state and the market place.

The gender analysis was designed and led by the author and was carried out by a team of two members. An NGO worker participated in the fieldwork and also assisted in translation, and field observations and clarifications which in turn helped in analysis, and write-up of the report. The Universe of the study was carried out in three Taungya villages of Saharanpur district. From these three clusters, sample sizes of 30 women each were selected randomly and informed consent was sought for being a respondent of the study. Participants were mainly the females who participated in the wage schemes run by Government of India like Mahatma Gandhi National Rural Employment Guarantee Act (MGNREGA) at each research village, approximately 30 respondents were a part of the research. Some of them participated in in-depth interviews, Focused Group Discussion (FGD) and Participatory Rural Appraisal (PRA) exercises. Participatory focused Group discussions were held separately with groups of women involved in the wage schemes. All interviews were recorded, and respondents gave informed consent prior to the discussions.

The questions in the interview schedule were structured around the application of PRA tools to facilitate discussion and participation of the respondents in the research process. The research focused mainly on the family/household, simultaneously analysing how gender norms and rules display at the institutional level of the market, work force participation and in selected community institutions like credit lending institutions and formal social participation in Gram Panchayat meetings or NGOs' meetings.

Discussion:

Development as increased well being: Focusing on associations between people and their association to resources and activities

Almost in all the Taungya villages, most of the women were involved in wage employment activities being run by the Forest Department. The rest of women are involved in livestock rearing and *Baan-making* (rope making). Apart from the wage employment works, women are involved in the afforestation works undertaken by the Forest Department for the rest of the year. Forest officials prefer women over the Taungya men due to their sincerity and commitment. A young married woman commented, "*Since us all women from the same village work in wage employment, we feel secure coming together and going back to work in forests together.*"

Since Taungya women have been involved in the Taungya system of cultivation so they are quite experts in the management of natural resources. This was the sole reason for their involvement in the afforestation activities of the Forest Department. Taungya women are also experts in the farming of different cropping patterns along with the afforestation activities. They have knowledge of which herb and shrub grows better under the shades of the trees leading to the maximisation of the land patterns. One thing that gets evident is that women tend to know more about the medicinal value of plants since they are the ones who indulge more in the forest peripheral areas. Again it is the young Taungya females who take their livestock for grazing so they are more aware of the 'good' and 'bad' areas around the place. They know precisely which are the forbidden areas in order to avoid the attack from wild animals like *neelgai,* wild elephants etc.

Institutional Analysis: (Revealing how these relationships reworked through Institutions such as the credit facilities)

In the Taungya community, women have access to both formal and informal credit networks. Wage employment schemes like MGNREGA has given them 'immediate income opportunity and seems to be changing the social fabric of the society.' Rani Devi says, "*Wage employment money has helped us in increasing our savings habit and it provides us with a financial security in lean periods. Earlier in labour works, we got wages on daily basis so there were no savings as the liquid income was used instantly in family expenditure.*" The villagers agreed that their savings in bank account has got them out of the clutches of moneylenders who gave them loans at higher rate of interests and at times, in cases of non-payment, they had to part ways with their livestock. So wage employment has on one hand enhanced their purchasing power and savings but has reduced their credit loans.

Taungya women although have all the autonomy of free mobility and workforce participation yet their social positioning is commanded greatly by the male counterparts of the Taungya community. On the contrary, women folk are not allowed to speak in the public forum and are allowed to be the mute spectators. Due to the emergence of schemes like wage employment which makes it mandatory for women participation in work and their presence in the proceedings of Gram Panchayat meetings, Taungya women have got a platform to get exposed to the formal proceedings of work force. But here too they are there for the very reason of being required there. The one most subjugating aspect of the male folk over the communication of female viewpoint is controlled to the extent that in the FGDs with the females, every time a question was posed to a woman, the answer came out of a male. E.g. a Female in one of the FGD emphasised that women under MGNREGA were being paid ₹ 80 against ₹ 120 paid to a male. She was instantly shrugged and asked to keep silence by the men folk. However, upon walking a bit of distance, the women folk followed the researcher and validated the fact given by that female.

Although the women still showed low social participation in the Gram Panchayat meetings, they seemed quite aware of their rights in wage employment. However, still the social conditions do not allow them to attend the meetings.

Social Relations and Social Transformations

In the Taungya community, it is the woman who takes care of the major household expenditure so she is the one to manage the finances. Taungya women are active in contributing to the family income as their formal workforce participation is high. Taungya women manage the finances of the household by having saving accounts in the Post Office. This economic independence has also led to changing of gender equations and relations within the family institutions. Taungya women reported that, *"My husband helps me in the household chores once I come back from work site and he looks after the children when I go for working in wage employment."*

The women opined that today they are in a better position to take decisions regarding their children's health and education as they also contribute to the household income. Their husband has begun to value their suggestions and mostly decisions are based on consensual understanding. However, it was reported in the FGDs that it was their husbands who operated their passbooks. There is a need to change the perception that "*we will get work when the Forest Department starts the afforestation drives.*" Since these villages are on the periphery of the forests, it is the Forest Department who assigns them wage employment works under the afforestation drives.

Underlining the distinctions and complications of Gender Relations

Women of Taungya community have social and religious standing which gives them the autonomy of free movement with no restrictions. As Taungya belong to Scheduled Castes category, their women folk enjoys a free intermingling of gender compare to higher castes in the region. Women in Taungya are free to visit their work sites, health-care facilities, relatives and market areas around the urban areas which are at least 10-15 kms away from their settlements. Taungya women travel to their worksite which is normally at the periphery of the forests where they need to travel on foot for at least 1-2 kms or by bus too. It is the Taungya women who normally carry an ailing child to the *Local vaidya* or a private doctor as the man of the family are involved in the labour works at distant township. Any kind of medical emergency is dealt by the Taungya females as they cannot afford to wait for their husbands to come back as they reach late in the night and are normally drunk. As their villages are settled villages on the periphery of forests, there is no provision of transportation reaching their villages so they have to walk on foot for at least 3-4 kms in order to reach their villages once they get down from the local transport connecting them to the urban centres. Taungya women normally form a group to visit the local *haats* and *melas* that are held on the festivals around their villages. The Taungya women who are not into the formal employment look after the livestock which is normally small ruminants. It is the women-folk who take them to the forests and the areas adjoining the forest for grazing purpose. Taungya women visit their relatives as and when required and she does not seek out for the permission of her husband or in-laws in doing so.

It is the Taungya women who take major decisions regarding the education and marriage of their sons and daughters. The general observation is that although they have meager say in the community-related matters but when it comes to the matters of the family life, it is the Taungya women who lead by example. Any household visited on fieldwork depicted a very harmonious relationship between the mother-in-law and daughter-in-laws.

In Taungya community, girls and boys are married at a young age so most of the daughters-in-laws were young girls who were treated like daughters in their in-laws house. The duty of a daughter-in-law was to just attend to the daily household chores. She was not allowed to join any formal work employment opportunity rather the mother-in-law would go for the work. The young daughter-in-law tends to small ruminants at home but never takes them out for grazing. It was amazing that despite being a female researcher; still young daughter-in-laws always offered water with a veil on their face. The reason sensed was owing to the male escorts with me. Mostly, it is the mother who emphasised on the education of both daughters and sons at the school within the village. As Taungya is a settled village so as part of the settlement plan of their village, they were given a primary school within one km of proximity. The results of the Taungya women passion towards education gets evident when our data showed almost 90 per cent of educated youth.

Outcomes of the Gender Analysis

The gender analysis process was followed with the key findings and identifying how they could be addressed and incorporated in the women empowerment strategy. The strategy, drawing from the gender analysis findings, identified the priority issues (as defined by the respondents), to be enhanced physical mobility, financial autonomy, low investment in assets like livestock, low voice on public forums, unequal decision-making power, unequal daily workload sharing, and prevalence of alcoholism and domestic violence. The strategy then acknowledged the transitional and fundamental norms or beliefs (from the research) that were used to give reason for and sustain these inequalities (for instance, 'women's work is considered dual with participation in formal workforce participation and at domestic front', or 'women are expected to contribute in the public employment domain but should be docile enough to not voice their concerns in public domains').

Chapter - 6

Sustainable Livelihood Strategies of Taungya

Livelihoods can be understood as "the assets (natural, physical, human, financial and social capital), the activities (strategies of use), and the access to these (mediated by institutions and social relations) that together determine the living gained by the individual and the household" (Ellis 2000: 10). In the context of resource dependent people livelihood and the related activities are best understood as a "way of life" (Rigg, 2005; Nayak and Berkes, 2011). 'Sustainable' then refers to the longer-term and 'livelihood' to the many activities which make up a living. By using the livelihood framework presented in annexure the different elements constituting assets, activities and livelihood strategies as well as the vulnerability context will constitute as the point of departure of the discussion.

The first step in this study of household livelihood analysis is to categorise livelihood strategies and understand how household well-being is related to each strategy. Livelihood strategies can easily be identified and characterised using well-being status.

According to the information obtained from the focus groups discussions in *Taungya* community, rich households own pucca house made of concrete brick and cement with a cemented roof. The medium households own a semi-pucca house made of brick and mud with no concrete roof. The poor households live in a thatched hut tenement made of mud.The rich households are mainly engaged in small enterprises and forest activities while the medium households engage in both wage employment and Baan-making. The poor households are only involved in wage employment.

Table 6.1: Well-being status defined according to the Taungya villagers (n=100)

	Rich	*Medium*	*Poor*	*Total*
Taungya	8(8)	70(70)	22(22)	100(100)

Sces of Livelihood of Taungya

Taungya households are migrated households from the state of West Bengal who rely on a combination of activities to meet their needs and to disperse risks. A wide range of resources and livelihood strategies are employed by Taungya households: migration, wage employment (regular and occasional), livestock rearing and forest activities. The significance of their traditional occupational pattern of multiple cropping is assessed below in the context of this wide array of livelihood strategies. The contribution of each economic activity, especially afforestation-related activities, to some of the needs is reviewed.

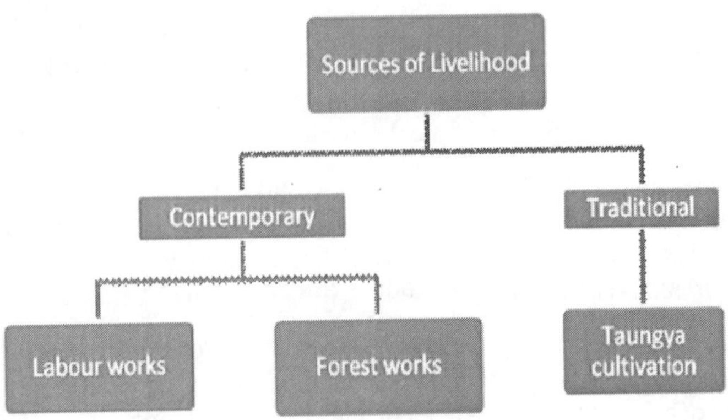

Fig. 6.1: Sources of livelihood of Taungya.

Contemporary Sources of Livelihood

(i) Labour works

Taungya households eke out much of their incomes from forests. As is shown in Table below, 46 per cent of the households were having either primary or secondary dependence on forest produce. Of them, 20 per cent were primary dependents and the rest 44 per cent were secondary dependents. Primary dependents were Taungyas who earned their primary income from afforestation activities or as forest guards. Secondary dependents were mainly into selling of *Bhabar grass* and use it for *Baan-making*.

Table 6.2: Alternate Livelihood Strategy of Participant and Non-participant Taungya

	Participants	*Non-Participants*	*Total*
Daily Wages	18(36)	26(52)	44(88)
Forest works	22(44)	0	22(44)
Sell bhabar grass	0	1(2)	1(2)
Daily wages and livestock	0	9(18)	9(18)
Wages and Baan-making	10(20)	14(28)	24(48)
Total	**50(100)**	**50(100)**	**100(200)**

Figures in parenthesis show percentages to their respective totals.

In the contemporary days, the villagers have received lots of option for their livelihoods. The emergence of stone mining industries has given a scope for moving out of village. The introduction of Mahatma Gandhi National Rural Employment Scheme (MGNREGS) has also brought some hope in the minds of poor tribals. The introduction of other development projects like Anthodia Scheme, BPL and Mahamaya acheme have widened their scope of livelihoods. It has reduced the rate of migration in the village. The villagers who used to go out of State in search of jobs have come back. At present, their world of migration is mostly confined to their block and locality. However, still majority of them are depending on agriculture as primary source of livelihood and they prefer working as agricultural labourers on other farmers fields.

Traditional Sources of Taungya Livelihood

If we look into the changing contest of livelihood of Kaluwala

Taungya village, it will be found that it has changed a lot in course of time. During the British period, the villagers were mostly depending on forest resources for their livelihoods. They used to collect various forest based products and fuel woods from nearby forest. The villagers were managing the forest. Apart from forest resources, they used to do some cultivation in forest land. Mostly, it was a system of multiple cropping. Their economy was subsistence in nature. They were struggling to feed them. In the due course of time, the study area witnessed lots of change. In 1985, the Taungya cultivation was abolished in the study area. The land allotted to them is on the periphery of the forests and is infected with *laltana* weed which makes it difficult for cultivation. To add to it further there is lack of irrigation facilities in the area.

(i) Forest as Livelihood Asset

Taungya is the only community which has primary dependence on forest engaged in collection and sales of non-timber forest produce. All the 100 Taungya respondent households in the study area depend on forest as their main source of income directly or indirectly. Being a forest-bound village, the rest of its population is also linked directly or indirectly to collection of forest produce in organising their livelihood activities, such as collection of firewood, green manure, green fodder etc. Taungyas depend on the forest for gathering food and food materials, such as tubers and yams. During some months wage work is also available related to forest maintenance, fire-line making, construction of check-dams and boundary posts, etc. undertaken by the Forest Department.

The labourers of the villages work on daily wages. The primary source of income of the labourers is daily wages. Labourer works in the MGNREGA for hundred days and when their hundred days are over, some of them work with the farmers of the adjoining villages and others migrate to cities like Saharanpur and Dehradun and work there. Some of the labour participants also have domestic animals like goats. They get milk from the goats as well as they get to sell the kids when they are six months old. A goat gives birth to three kids at one time. Taungya labourers do own a small piece of land and they do agriculture work as well as work as a daily wage labour in the village. The labour participants owning the land informed that their land condition is not good and they get very less production out of it. They donot have any irrigation facilities on their land. Hence, the participants consider this as secondary source of income. The participant labourers told that their all family members work as a daily wage labour either in the government work (in the MGNREGA) or other manual labour work such as agriculture work with the farmers or stone-breaking machines which are running in the village for producing sand from rock.

Daily wage labour work is not enough for the labourers hence both the working class are trying to generate income from other sources also. This is the clear evidence that, neither farmer is happy with his agriculture production nor the labourer is happy with the daily wage rate which he receives from the farmers. Therefore, both the working class is working extra to fill the gap in the earning. The labourers first complete their hundred days in the MGNREGA after that only they work with the farmers of the village because after hundred days they don't have any choice to work in the village. Some of the labourers also migrate towards the cities like Saharanpur and Dehradun because they are not happy with the wage rate which is paid by the farmers of the village. The labourers who cannot go outside for work, work with the farmers in the village.

In this part of our study, we discuss the livelihood activities pursued by households and their outcomes as related to asset base. The activities they pursue are the result of their livelihood strategies. Assets and endowments of households help them shape individual livelihoods while vulnerabilities push households to seek and pursue coping strategies. Natural capital, human capital, physical capital, financial capital and social capital are the five-dimensional asset base of households. Land, education, housing pattern, investments and credit facilities and participation in organisational activities are taken as proxies for them. Occupational patterns are described in detail in order to bring out the mosaic of livelihood activities. The monthly per capita consumption expenditure (MPCE) of households are assumed to quantify livelihood outcomes.

Diversification in Livelihood due to Push Factors

Lack of permanent settlement: According to Harris (1972), the major problem with Taungya system in most regions is that the land remains under the ownership of the government or commercial enterprises. The farmers' desire for outright land ownership is often frustrated. Living in abject poverty and deprived of the basic constitutional rights, Taungyas were used by the forest department (FD) for over 60 years as bonded labourers to regenerate forests but now have been declared as encroachers on the same land (Tripathy A, 2011). Owning a piece of land and achieving permanent settlement is the ultimate goal of most Taungya farmers in an agriculturally based society. This gives the Taungya farmers an intimate relationship with the land. Gajaseni (1988) observed that lack of permanent settlement, under-employment, and low productivity are problems for the rural poor which cannot be solved by the earlier approaches to Taungya. He also reported that some of the problems have been partially overcome by the modern Forest Village Taungya in Thailand, in which rural farmers live in houses subsidised by the government and private industries. The farmers are permitted to cultivate food crops during the early years of the plantations, and are given wages for silvicultural labour.

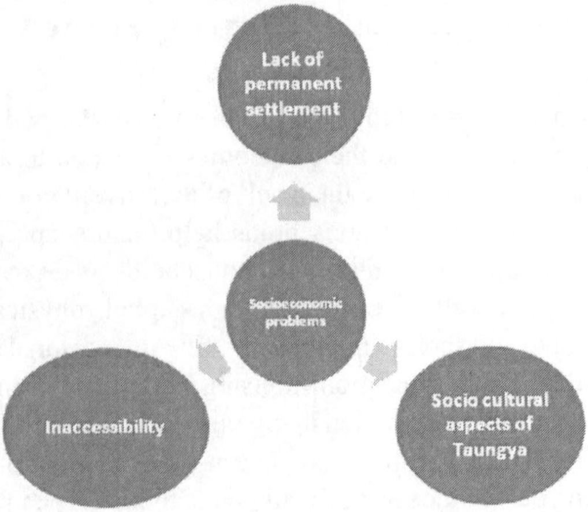

Fig. 6.2: Socio-economic problems with Taungya.

Inaccessibility: Taungya villages are settled villages at the periphery of the forests meant for afforestation activities. The trees were planted in a nursery bed and the growth of the forest, the land allotted to them was surrounded by planted trees which made it more prone to wild animals.

Socio-cultural aspects of Taungya: Gajaseni (1990) experienced that Forest Village Taungya was compatible with the prevailing local values and customs. The Taungyas in Uttar Pradesh have adapted to the lifestyle of the adjoining areas and their cultural life could in no way demarcate them from being an immigrants from West Bengal.

He also ascertained that three major improvements are required for the system to be permanently successful. These are;

(i) ensuring permanent settlement,

(ii) increasing income earning opportunities,

(iii) developing supportive facilities such as school and health centres.

Access to Assets for Livelihood in Taungya Community

Natural Capital

Livestock keeping

Livestock resources play a key role in livelihoods, not only as a source of cash income from the sale of livestock and livestock products such as milk and raw leather but also as a source of protein for villagers themselves, and as a source of manure and compost for agricultural use.The study indicates the estimated livestock population being kept by Taungya farmers in the study area. The kinds of livestock being kept include sheep, goat, poultry and/or cattle. Sheep constituted about 19 per cent, goats 18 per cent, poultry 62 per cent and cattle one per cent of the total number of livestock being raised by Taungya farmers.

Table 6.3: Livestock keeping of Taungya (n=50)

Number of livestock	*Status*			*Total*
	Poor	*Medium*	*Rich*	
0-5	11(22)	30(60)	3(6)	44(88)
5-10	0	5(10)	1(2)	6(12)
Total	**11(22)**	**35(70)**	**4(8)**	**50(100)**
Gamma= .730, significant = .069				

Source: Based on field survey (2012).

Figures in parenthesis show percentages to their respective totals.

The cross-tabulation between number of livestock and well-being status demonstrates that the relationship between two variables is weak (G = .730) as well as statistically insignificant (Sig= .069).

Field Observation: The Taungya farmers in the study area do not combine the livestock directly with the established Taungya plantations but rather raise and keep them in the house, some in fenced structures made of teak slaps from sawmills. Occasionally, the livestock when released go to nearby taungya plantations and graze the under-story weeds in the plantations. Grazing the under-story weeds helps check the incidence of fire hazards to some degree by reducing the volume of flammable herbaceous plants. The livestock occasionally serve as source of protein for the household and also as additional source of income for the participating families. Nineteen per cent of the 160 farmers interviewed depend on the sales of livestock to carry out their household activities. Another reason is no one peasant depends exclusively on goat farming for their livelihood in this case study, while they were dependent on other livelihood activities like rainfed farming, daily wages to urban area as well as MGNREGA at local. Thus, most important aspect is that most of Taungyas take it as a subsidiary and additional income sources, not a commercial entity. In extensive goat production system, grazing of goat is a cornerstone activity. In this activity, old aged people of household, kids and very low proportion of adults has been contributed as human resources particularly open grazing of goats. The open grazing is a source of employment for unskilled people. In contrary, the open grazing has spoiled life of many of young kids who never ever go to school in their life owing to goat grazing. Most of the Taungyas emphasise that Goat-keeping helps in improving nutritional value of diet as goat milk is recommended by experts for infant and lactating mother because it is nutritive and easy to digest for kids. In rural setting, most of people do not buy milk because of lack of access to market and lack of purchase capacity particularly among the poor.

Table 6.4: Use of goat milk at household level

Particulars	*Number of respondents*	*Proportion (%)*
use in domestic purposes	40	83
we sell milk at dairy	8	17

Table 6.4 clearly explained that goat milk is being used by 83 per cent goat peasant's HH for domestic purposes and remaining 17 per cent goat peasants are sold at local private dairy. In other words, the milk has been utilised to drink for children and lactating women as most of poor peasants cannot buy milk from market. In subsequently, the goat milk helps in enhance nutritional status among vulnerable segment. This data supported best goat peasant interview that the interviewee elaborated that 'at my home, at first we often make tea and drink goat milk, and remaining milk we sell at dairy' Thus, the goat milk is a supplementary source to provide nutritional requirement among poor households.

Human Asset

Education

Human assets increase in proportion to the educational achievements of households. Education and skills become decisive variables for occupational diversification of household members. Moreover, productivity of workers is affected by the variables education and age.

It is seen from the Table 6.5 that more than two-fifth of the workers in the study area are illiterate and that about one-fifth of them are in the age group 15 to 25 years. Thus, it is clear that large-scale illiteracy prevails even among young workers.

Table 6.5: Participation of Taungya children in formal education (n=50)

Level of education	*Status*			*Total*
	Poor	*Medium*	*Rich*	
Illiterate	4(8)	0	1(2)	5(10)
Neoliterates	7(14)	10(20)	3(6)	20(40)
Primary	0	25(50)	0	25(50)
Total	**11(22)**	**35(70)**	**4(8)**	**50(100)**
Gamma= .473, significant = .042				

Source: Based on field survey (2012).

Figures in parenthesis show percentages to their respective totals.

The cross-tabulation between level of education and well-being status demonstrates that the relationship between two variables is strong (G = .473) as well as statistically significant (Sig= .042).

Field Observation: Illiteracy is the highest among tribal workers who have the least capability for occupational diversification. Only 60 per cent of the workers have education up to the Primary level and above. The reason behind this is that the population falling within the age group of 30 and above are mostly educated till primary levels. This population got settled with their parents in the settled Taungya village and as their parents were involved in Taungya plantation, the children went to the primary school constructed in every Taungya village as a part of the settlement plan.

Financial Asset

Credit facilities available to the Households

Taungya depend mainly on informal networks of credit facilities through relatives (25 per cent), friends (5 per cent) and moneylenders (66 per cent) who charge exorbitant interests for the emergency loans lent out to Taungya community. Members work as daily wagers and have no access to basic facilities such as education and health. Their names are in electoral rolls but do not exist in revenue records, hence they cannot get below poverty line cards or domicile certificates and donot qualify as guarantors for bank loans and bail in legal cases. Credit facilities are a distant dream for Taungya community owing to the inaccessibility of permanent resident address and also owing to the physical proximity of the banks being out of their purview.

Table 6.6: Credit facilities available to the Taungya Households (n=50)

Amount of Credit	*Status*			*Total*
	Poor	*Medium*	*Rich*	
< 2000	11(22)	34(68)	3(6)	48(96)
2000-5001	0	1(2)	0	1(2)
>5001	0	0	1(2)	1(2)
Total	**11(22)**	**35(70)**	**4(8)**	**50(100)**
Gamma= .900, significant = .232				

Source: Based on field survey (2012).

Figures in parenthesis show percentages to their respective totals.

The cross-tabulation between sources of amount of credit and well-being status demonstrates that the relationship between two variables is weak (G = .900) as well as statistically insignificant (Sig=.232).

Field Observation: One reason for the increase in the number of loans appears to be the need for meeting essential expenditure in the face of the steep decline in income caused by fall in prices of farm produce. Another reason could have been the strategy of banks of allowing conversion of old unpaid debts into new debts. Easy access to credit facilities for Taungya farmers would enable them to improve their methods of cultivation and to store, process, and sell their produce at the right time to obtain maximum profit. Credit facilities are also necessary to enable farmers to acquire improved farm inputs, such as fertilisers, herbicides, and farm machinery.

Physical Assets

Sources of lighting

The mains electricity supply has a profound effect on structural development and improves the quality of life of the population of any country. It brings significant economic progress into rural areas, for example in the form of micro and small-scale enterprises, which in addition to providing the owners with new income, also create employment for many people. Unfortunately, this study area has not yet been supplied with mains electricity. But some of the better off and middle class families use solar panels from the national NGOs, named RLEK. This is a very good alternative energy source but FGD participants state that the solar energy panels are quite expensive and poor people cannot afford them.

Table 6.7: Sources of lighting of Taungya Household (n=50)

Sources of lighting	***Status***			***Total***
	Poor	***Medium***	***Rich***	
Fuelwood	0	5(10)	0	5(10)
Kerosene	11(22)	27(54)	4	42(84)
Solar lamps	0	3(6)	0	3(6)
Total	**11(22)**	**35(70)**	**4**	**50(100)**
Gamma= -.117, significant = .503				

Source: Based on field survey (2012).

Figures in parenthesis show percentages to their respective totals.

The cross-tabulation between sources of of lighting and well-being status demonstrates that the relationship between two variables is weak (G = .851) as well as statistically insignificant (Sig=.503).

Field Observation: According to researcher, this is because of the farmers have large amount of land, they can produce fodder from their land or they can buy from elsewhere since they can afford it. But labourers don't have land so they cannot get fodder for their animals therefore they rear goats. Rearing goats is not hard work because the goat eat very less as compare to cow. The labourers also collect firewood every day for fuel. They get leaves with the wood and take it home so that their goat can be fed. A goat gives birth to three kids at one time and cow only gives one kid in a year therefore the poor people can earn soon through selling goat in the market.

Social Asset

Participation in Social Organisation

Social organisations refer to institutions, relationships, and norms that shape the quality and quantity of a society's social interactions.

For quantifying the participation rate of people in social organisations, the percentages of population aged 15 years and above to the total population aged 15 years and above in the study area were considered. From the survey it was found that local village informal panchayats are the major social organisation of the people; next in the order comes religious institutions. Nearly 50 per cent of the households which participate in informal village Panchayat activities are casual agricultural labourers and about one-third olderly women. The same participation pattern is found in the case of religious institutions also.

The cross-tabulation between level of social participation and well-being status demonstrates that the relationship between two variables is strong (G = 1.000) as well as statistically insignificant (Sig= .009).

Field Observation: The level of social interaction among tribals is poor. However, they participate in MGNREGA activities. Taungyas have no voice in running the society. Forests near to Taungyas are poor in so far as forest produce is concerned. In political organisations and trade unions Taungyas do not participate; a fact which indicates that their social interaction and networks are poor. Participation in recreational activities is restricted to the festivals and social gatherings like Haats or melas.

Table 6.8: Level of social participation of the Taungya Households (n=50)

Level of social participation	*Status*			*Total*
	Poor	*Medium*	*Rich*	
No participation	11(22)	33 (66)	0	44(88)
Informal participation	0	2(4)	3(6)	5(10)
Formal participation	0	0	1(2)	1(2)
Total	**11(22)**	**35 (70)**	**4(8)**	**50**

Gamma= 1.000, significant = .009

Source: Based on field survey (2012).

Figures in parenthesis show percentages to their respective totals.

Box 6.1: A Summary of Livelihood Strategies of Taungya

Coping	*Intensification*	*Extensification*	*Migration*	*Diversification*
• Take loans and credit • Mortgage and sell assets • Change in food habits • Discontinue children's education • Rearrange personal and professional Relationships	• Grass selection and use • Stop seasonal labour works (no longer following traditional seasonal labour works) • No time and space restriction	• Travel long distances for cutting *Bhabar* grass • Look beyond the *Baan* making • Product extensification	• Outmigration to distant towns and adjoining work sites	• Activities linked to primary Occupation (multiple cropping along with subsistence farming) • Use of available natural capital (private land assets): Creating future assets for income generation • Host of non-labour occupations • Engage women and children in income generation

Livelihood Strategies of Taungya

In the due course of time, the study area witnessed lots of change. In 1985, the Taungya cultivation was abolished in the study area. The land allotted to them is on the periphery of the forests and is infected with laltana weed which makes it difficult for cultivation. To add to it further there is lack of irrigation facilities in the area. These conditions compelled Taungya for adoption of various livelihood strategies.

Livelihood Diversification

Due to a general lack of options and start up finances, livelihood diversification has not been a very successful strategy amongst Taungya.

The Table 6.9 shows that the maximum 70 per cent of participant Taungya opted for engage women and children in income generation. Almost 16 per cent went for use of available natural resources followed by host of non-labour occupations (10 per cent) and activities linked to primary occupation. Amongst the Non-participant Gujjar, activities linked to primary occupation (76 per cent) followed by host of non-labour occupations and engage women and children in income generation are the intensification strategy followed maximum (10 per cent). Table below lists the various livelihood diversification strategies of Taungya:

Table 6.9: Diversification Strategies for Livelihood Subsistence in Taungya

	Diversification strategies for livelihood subsistence	*Participant Taungya*	*Nonparticipant Taungya*	*Total*
(i)	Activities linked to primary Occupation	2 (4)	38 (76)	40
(ii)	Use of available natural resources	8 (16)	2 (4)	10
(iii)	Host of non-labour occupations	5 (10)	5 (10)	10
(iv)	Engage women and children in income generation	35 (70)	5 (10)	40
	Total	**50 (100)**	**50 (100)**	**100**

Figures in parenthesis show percentages to their respective totals.

As part of their strategy for livelihood diversification, Taungya households take up several activities which are discussed here under three broad categories. First, households engage in a number of activities that are linked to their primary or only occupation, which is farming. While men have opted for employment on private agricultural lands as labourers, women have taken up to afforestation activities in the Forest Department. Second, a number of households chose a host of non-farming activities as part of livelihood diversification strategy. Activities such as front door retail shops, shops in the village or nearby market places, daily wage, salaried jobs (private and government), the sale of fruits from household trees and raising animals are part of this strategy. Third, several households make use of available natural resources, primarily land, in an effort to create future assets for income generation. If successful it can offer a stable source of income to a small number of households in the Taungya villages even though this is more of a long-term strategy for livelihood diversification. Activities under this strategy include vegetable growing and poultry farming.

Box 6.2: Livelihood Diversification Substrategies for Taungya

Diversification as a livelihood strategy	*Sub-strategy Activity*
Activities linked to primary Occupation (multiple cropping along with subsistence farming)	Afforestation activities Labour works involved in the agricultural sector Drying of the *Bhabbar grass* Employment in the Forest Department as a watchman
Use of available natural resources (private land assets): Creating future assets for income generation	Poultry rearing Vegetable cultivation Tree plantation on homestead
Host of non-labour occupations	Selling fruit from fruit trees at backyard Open retail shops in the village Daily wage Salaried private jobs Rearing goats
Engage women and children in income generation	Women engage in several occupations Adolescent children engage in livelihood related occupations

Table above illustrates that even after years of livelihood crisis and a staggering loss of incomes after banning of Taungya plantation works, most households in the study villages continue to retain plantation works either as their primary or the only livelihood occupation. In this context, it is interesting to observe what makes diversification of livelihood activities difficult in the context of Taungya farmers? Since these are Scheduled Caste who have for generations not done anything else other than Taungya cultivation, they tend to lack the necessary skills and resources to take up alternate livelihood activities. Even though locally available options for livelihood are limited, what is available does not fit the existing skill levels of the Taungya households. This makes the diversification of livelihood activities outside the forest sector difficult to pursue. Diversification remains a "mental block" for several Taungya households who consider Taungya farming as a caste or cultural activity, a way of life, rather than an economic pursuit. This complicates livelihood choices further in terms of people moving out of farming to non-farming activities. The "mental block" not only comes from a sense of cultural connection to the Taungya farming but also results from their fear of moving away from their traditional farming as a way of life to a completely different way of life. Many old Taungyas think that by being born into a Taungya community, they are solemnly tied to Taungya farming as their identity.

Field Observation: Field observations illustrates that even after years of livelihood crisis and a staggering loss of incomes, banning of taungya plantation works, most households in the study villages continue to retain plantation works either as their primary or the only livelihood occupation. In this context, it is interesting to observe what makes diversification of livelihood activities difficult in the context of Taungya farmers? Since these are *Chamars* (scheduled) by caste, who have for generations not done anything else other Taungya cultivation, they tend to lack the necessary skills and resources to take up alternate livelihood activities. Even though locally available options for livelihood are limited, what is available does not fit the existing skill levels of the Taungya households. This makes the diversification of livelihood activities outside the forest sector difficult to pursue. Diversification remains a "mental block" for several Taungya households who consider Taungya farming as a caste or cultural activity, a way of life, rather than an economic pursuit.

This complicates livelihood choices further in terms of people moving out of farming to non-farming activities. The "mental block" not only comes from a sense of cultural connection to the Taungya farming but also results from their fear of moving away from their traditional farming as a way of life to a completely different way of life. Many old Taungyas think that by being born into a fishing caste, they are solemnly tied to Taungya farming as their identity.

Coping Strategies for Livelihood Subsistence

For the poor Taungya households, a livelihood crisis often impacts the existing support system for subsistence. Consider that 100 per cent of households in both the study villages said they preferred to make arrangements to address immediate subsistence needs on a priority basis before any long-term strategy was even considered. This would ensure some level of basic livelihood security in maintaining access to food, healthcare, education for children and social relationships.

The findings of the study show that the maximum almost 60 per cent of participant Taungya opted for taking loans and credit. Almost 16 per cent went for change in food habits followed by mortgage and selling assets (14 per cent) and discontinuing children's education (6 per cent). Amongst the Nonparticipant Taungya, taking loans and credit (60 per cent) followed by mortgage and selling assets (30 per cent) and change in food habits (4 per cent).

Table 6.10: Coping Strategies for Livelihood Subsistence in Taungya

	Coping strategies for Livelihood subsistence	***Participant Taungya***	***Non-participant Taungya***
(i)	Take loans and credit	30(60)	30(60)
(ii)	Mortgage and sell assets	7(14)	15(30)
(iii)	Change in food habits	8(16)	2(4)
(iv)	Discontinue children's education	3(6)	1(2)
(v)	Rearrange personal and professional Relationships	2(4)	2(4)
	Total	**50(100)**	**50(100)**

Figures in parenthesis show percentages to their respective totals.

As Table 6.10 illustrates, most of these subsistence strategies were relatively easy to access and doable; however not without long-term implications. The following section tries to outline some of these problems: how a number of households fell into a vicious debt trap and the resulting financial uncertainties.

Box 6.3: Livelihood Coping Substrategies for Taungya

Coping strategies for livelihood subsistence	*Sub-strategy Activity*
Take loans and credit	Consumption loans from multiple sources Cash advance from petty traders Credit from village grocery store
Mortgage and sell assets	Mortgage and sell of household items. Mortgage of household equipments.
Change in food habits	Low quality and quantity of food
Discontinue children's education	Some sent elder children to work
Rearrange personal and professional Relationships	Break away from joint family Send elder children to live with relatives in other villages

Accessing financial asset had a significant role in determining how a household could deal effectively with some of the initial challenges posed by livelihood crisis. It was also a factor for preparing the household to undertake more long-term strategies to move from coping to other livelihood strategies. In their pursuit of immediate coping strategies, Taungya households mostly went after accessing available financial asset in the form of loans, advances and credits. Taungyas of Bhagwatpur went to the moneylender for small cash loans on each of those days when he failed to get a daily labour work. With falling employment opportunities, they now do this for more than ten days a month. Taungyas consider cash loans as critical to ensure a supply of food to his family, whilst trying out other options for a more reliable income. Taungyas go for mortgaging of household items and household equipments in dire crisis. As a last resort, Taungya families tend to send their elder children away to relatives place.

Intensification Strategies

Intensification becomes inevitable as most of these households approach a point of saturation in terms of pursuing immediate coping strategies for subsistence. As among intensification strategy, the Taungyas intensify their afforestation and *Baan-making* activities to make the most of resources available under the given socio-ecological conditions. In both Khushalpur and Sodinagar, the bulk of intensification occurs within the Goat rearing sector and in Kaluwala Taungya village, *Baan-making* acts as an intensification strategy. Table outlines various sub-strategies and activities pursued by Taungyas for intensification in all the study villages. Forest Department are often forthcoming if households want to stay on afforestation activities, or want to come back to it after periods of staying away from forestation works as the Forest Department relies on the knowledge of the Taungya farmers in Taungya plantation works. This knowledge helps the department in carrying out its afforestation drive more efficiently. This also works as an incentive for many households to cling on to forestation works and gradually intensify and extensify their efforts even though this may not be sufficient.

Table 6.11: Intensification Strategies for Livelihood Subsistence in Taungya

	Intensification strategies for livelihood subsistence	*Participant Taungya (n=50)*	*Non-participant Taungya*
(i)	Grass selection and use	21(42)	40(80)
(ii)	Stop seasonal labour works	15(30)	0
(iii)	No time and space restriction	14(28)	10(20)
	Total	**50 (100)**	**50 (100)**

Figures in parenthesis show percentages to their respective totals.

The findings of the Table above shows that the maximum almost 42 per cent of participant Taungya opt for grass selection and use. thirty per cent go for stop seasonal labour works followed by no time and space restriction (28 per cent). Amongst the Non-participant Taungya, Grass selection and use (80 per cent) followed by no time and space restriction (20 per cent).

Field observations show that with intensification most of the customary systems of *Baan-making* have changed significantly. Discussions with the elderly Taungyas revealed that earlier *Baan-making* was a year round livelihood strategy but since few years, *Bhabar* grass is allowed to be sold only during September to November months so this decision of the Forest Department has restricted this activity to being a seasonal livelihood strategy. After the onset of the livelihood crisis, intensification strategies included interfering with this seasonality in order to maximise on profits accrued out of the *Baan-making*. The new strategies led to the buying of the Bhabar grass through the mafias who steal the grass from the forest irrespective of the season and permission of the Forest Department. The new techniques enabled households to make *Baan* year round, disregarding seasonality. Most of these ropes are made and marketed throughout the year, in contrast to the original seasonality of only two to four months. Earlier, under a regime of customary *Baan-making*, norms evolved by the communities offered safeguards to different species of grass and the *Baan-making* season was the time of merriment for the community. However, *Baan-making* intensification brought in strategies that by default removed the customary restrictions on the size, species, time and location of the forest resources. Goat keeping is an alternate strategy for livelihoods.

Box 6.4: Livelihood Intensification Substrategies for Taungya

Intensification as livelihood strategy	*Sub-strategy Activity*
Grass selection and use	Select *Bhabar* grass of fine mess size. Use labour intensive techniques for making fine ropes
Stop seasonal labour works (no longer following traditional seasonal labour works)	Year-round labour works of all available semiskills.
No time and space restriction	Labour works anytime anywhere Semi-permanent and permanent Goat keeping

Extensification

Extensification is practised as a strategy to include more productive areas of the forest under *Baan-making* and to also convert strategically located cultivable lands into farm lands. Other strategies of extensification are listed in Table below:

Table 6.12: Extensification Strategies for Livelihood Subsistence in Taungya

Extensification Strategies for Livelihood Subsistence	***Participant Taungya***	***Non-participant Taungya***
(i) Travel long distances for cutting *Bhabar grass*	2(4)	23(46)
(ii) Look beyond the *Baan-making*	8(16)	22(44)
(iii) Product extensification	40(80)	5(10)
Total	**50(100)**	**50(100)**

Figures in parenthesis show percentages to their respective totals.

The finding of the table above shows that 16 per cent of participant Taungya opted for product extensification. Almost 80 per cent went for looking beyond the *Baan*-making followed by travelling long distances for cutting *Bhabar grass* (four per cent). Amongst the Non-participant Taungya, travelling long distances for cutting *Bhabar grass* (46 per cent) was followed by looking beyond the *Baan-making* (44 per cent) and product extensification(10 per cent).

Box 6.5: Livelihood Extensification Substrategies for Taungya

Extensification as a livelihood strategy	***Sub-strategy Activity***
Travel long distances for cutting *Bhabar* grass	Poaching outside traditional *Bhabar* cutting boundaries
Look beyond the *Baan-making*	Networks with the Traders buying ropes for urban areas Getting employment in the Saharanpur coir industry
Product extensification	Sale of raw *baan* ropes Products prepared from the ropes Use of herbal colours for the colouration of the ropes

Field observations show that a sharp decline in the free sale of *Bhabar* grass by the Forest Department have forced households to look for alternate areas of livelihood. This implies that average Taungya households now travel longer distances and often have to deal with the *mafias* who illegally cut the *bhabar* grass. This has led to poaching into the areas which lie outside the traditional proximity of the *Bhabar* cutting boundaries. At these locations, Taungyas have to not only face strong competition from the competing coir industry. As a strategy, they have begun to encash on their *Baan-making* skills by getting employed in the nearby coir industries of Saharanpur. This is considered a form of extensification that results in Taungyas now competing to capture several strategic areas within the skill set. In the same field, Taungyas have extended their strategy to product extensification. They sell the raw ropes and have begun to explore into various products like cots and chairs made of rope. Taungyas now make use of herbal colour. Thus, extensification as a strategy has multiple manifestations in the context of Taungya.

Migration

In the two study villages, there is not a single evidence of "moving away" (either individually or with family) and in each of the cases where migration has occurred, Taungya farmers have retained homes and families in the community and they return on a regular basis, some more frequently than others. Migration is a livelihood strategy for the Taungyas who could not get employment in MGNREGA works or in the forest works so they migrate to distant townships of Dehradun and Saharanpur for labour works. As the Table below enumerates that 20 per cent migrating Taungyas opted for being agricultural labourers, 30 per cent take up working on the construction sites, 6 per cent opt for self employment and 44 per cent turn into regular labourers in coir industry in the neighbouring townships.

Table 6.13: Nature of Work of the Taungya Migrant Labourers

Nature of work	*Migrating Taungya*
Agricultural labourers	20
Construction work	30
Self-employed	6
Regular labour	44
Total	**100**

Box 6.6: Field Note

MGNREGA combined with Seasonal Migration as Livelihood Strategy

Kishorilal of Bhagwatpur migrated to Dehradun for the first time in 2007 as a construction labour. He returned after a couple of months realising that he could do this for a few months per year and it was not a good idea to stay away from home indefinitely. Two years later Kishori manages to combine seasonal migration with MGNREGA works and other local activities to earn a livelihood for his family. He takes up new loans but he is also able to repay some of that in time, and he hopes to continue his current livelihood strategies with seasonal migration as an important component of it.

Source: Personal Communication.

Box 6.7: Livelihood Migration Substrategies for Taungya

Migration as a livelihood strategy	*Sub-strategy Activity*
Long-term migration	Migrate for indefinite period of time
Seasonal migration	Seasonal migration (for wage labour) becoming part of the annual cycle of livelihoods
Migrate within the state	Most migrate within Uttarakhand.
Migrate outside the state	Very few migrate outside the state.

In other words, if a Taungya had migrated due to the burden of debt then he may be inclined to return home once repayment of the debt has been done. Furthermore, the negligible earnings from migration by Taungya households suggests that the levels of income from migration are so low that it is neither possible to repay their debts and compensate for the loss of income from farming, nor make alternate arrangements for the lack of employment opportunities locally, all of which triggered migration in the first place. In addition to the factors outlined above, there are other constraints, such as uncertainties attached to migrating to an unknown place, which restrict Taungyas from pursuing out-migration as a more long-term and reliable livelihood strategy. Not all households are in a position to afford out-migration; households with many adult men are in an advantageous position compared to those with fewer adult men. As out-migration often involves traveling outside the state boundary for unspecified periods of time, many Taungya households with single men find it difficult to opt for it as a livelihood strategy. However, households with many young men tend to rely more on out-migration as a livelihood strategy when compared to households with elderly men.

There was no instance of migration by women or, except for one or two cases, migration with family members in the Taungya villages. Households that are part of an extended family were found to be more out-migration dependant than households consisting of nuclear families. Although only men migrated, the cost and effect of their migration on sending remittances back to families were profound. In the absence of men, the household stopped farming because culturally it was only men who farmed. Consequently, women in the household also discontinued their household chores and have taken to MGNREGA works and afforestation works with the Forest Department. Thus, out-migration by men also contributed to the disconnection of those family members who stay behind, from their customary farming resources.

Livelihood Pentagon Analysis

For analysing the access of people to various assets, the 'asset pentagon' technique has been used. The asset pentagon as in Figure 6.3 lies at the core of the livelihoods framework 'within' the vulnerability context. The pentagon is developed to provide information about people's assets to be presented visually, thereby bringing to life important interrelationships among the various assets. The shape of the pentagon can be used to show schematically variations in people's access to assets. The idea is that the central point of the pentagon, at which the lines meet, represents zero access to assets while the outer perimeter represents the maximum access to assets. So pentagons of different shapes will apply to different situations and these pentagons change over time. So the asset pentagon should be considered a dynamic presentation of the assets of a social group. On this basis pentagons of different shapes can be drawn for different communities or different social groups within the same communities.

To compare the sustainable development of both the communities, an Index was developed based on the indicators of five assets. For example, in the variable of Human Asset of education, scores were assigned on the scale of 1 to 3 on the basis of literacy levels, assigning the highest score when the respondent was literate and least to illiterate. For each activity, the scores were then multiplied by the number of respondents under respective education category, which were then summed up and converted on the scale of 3 and were named as 'scores'.

The index was then evolved by dividing the average scores for participant/non-participant for all activities by three.

The status of livelihoods in each village summarised in terms of pentagon depicts the five assets; Natural, Human, Social, Physical and Financial by calculating percentages of key indicators:

Table 6.14: Index indicating Accessibility of Taungya to Livelihood Asset Base

Asset Indices	***Participant Taungya***	***Nonparticipant Taungya***
Natural	.68	.68
Social	.69	.68
Physical	**.60**	**.31**
Financial	.65	.49
Human	**.83**	**.82**
Overall	.69	.59
Gain in Index value	**.1**	

The Index shows that Participant Gujjar have maximum access to natural asset but a medium access to Human, Social and Physical assets while the lowest access of participant Gujjar is to Financial asset. Non-participant Gujjar have highest access to Natural asset with medium access to Social, Human and financial asset while the lowest access of non-participant Gujjar is to Physical asset.

The Index shows that both participant and non-participant Taungya have maximum access to Human asset but a medium access to Financial, Social and Natural assets. The accessibility has been depicted in the Pentagons given below:

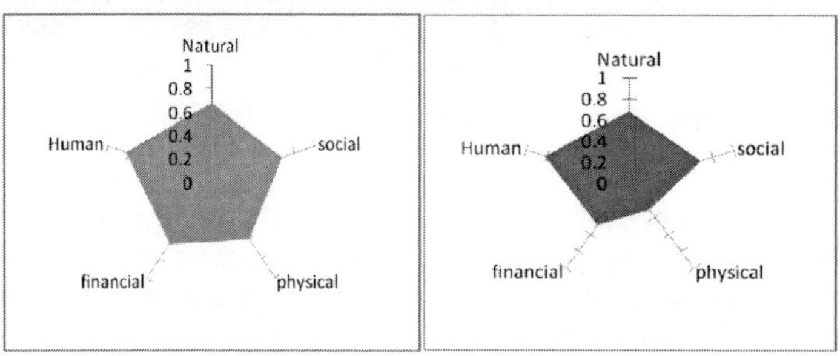

Participant Taungya *Non-participant Taungya*

Fig. 6.3: Livelihood Pentagons depicting Asset Accessibility in Taungya community.

Amongst Taungya community, Human asset is high for both participant and non-participant Taungyas due to the presence of a primary school within close quarters. Natural capital (98 per cent) and social assets are also substantial. Physical and Financial asset are high for Participant Taungya due to greater mobility to adjoining townships for labour works on daily basis and also accessibility to formal banking system owing to MGNREGA accounts. For the Participant Taungya, the pentagon is almost symmetrical due to the access to the employment opportunities, educational institution, active social participation in Gram Panchayat meetings held for MGNREGA, daily visits to nearby worksites and greater access to formal banking institutions.

Non-participant Taungya have low access to physical and financial assets due to low availability of employment and hence no access to financial institutions. Hence, the pentagon is highly asymetrical.

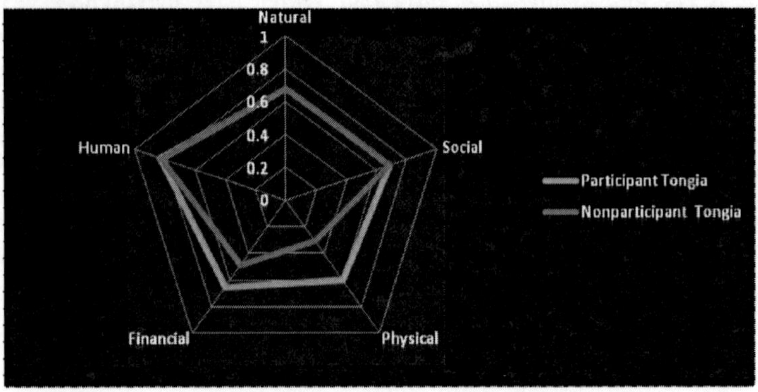

Fig. 6.4: Livelihood Pentagons depicting Accessibility to the Asset base in Taungya community.

Here Pentagon analysis depicts that the pentagon of non-participant Taungyas is less symmetrical showing low levels of accessibility to Asset base. This shows Non-participant Taungya are most vulnerable as have least access to all the assets whereas Participant Taungyas shows more symmetrical pentagon with higher accessibility levels to all the assets.

Chapter - 7

Conclusion

Taungya are the SC community living on the peripheries of the forest in settled villages and earn their livelihood through forest and daily labour works. Taungya communities are migrated labourers from West Bengal during British period. These communities face severe financial and economic distress owing to landlessness and are economically hard pressed.

Although the literacy among the Taungya was higher as compared to other communities, there level of literacy above primary education need to be enhanced. The Open Schooling Distance Education System may be popularised by establishing study centres in this Taungya dominated village.

There is tremendous requirement of improving the access of Taungya community to sanitation and safe drinking water and use of safe fuel for cooking. There is a need for provision of community toilets in settled Taungya villages and the provision of subsidised cooking fuel facilities will reduce the use of firewood among the Gujjar and Taungya which causes Asthma and eye diseases among them. Fuel wood requirements could be tackled through the installation of improved cooking stoves, biogas plants, subsidised LPG, and various other means at the village level.

Health status of this community is very low, therefore, Government/NGO working in this area should organise mobile immunisation and health check up camps on a monthly basis. Special mobile van facilities for lifting critical cases near the khols/Taungya villages to the referrel hospitals shall help in reduction of infant and maternal deaths.

Provision of infrastructure and support for improved agricultural practices as well as other natural resource based activities like apiculture would ensure better income to these poor households. Technical training should be provided to improve knowledge and skills in cultivating crops, livestock rearing and fish culture so that greater benefits accrue from proper utilisation of land.

Taungya women are participating in formal workforce which empowers them with decision-making and saving potential. Therefore, mahila mandals and microfinancing through Self Help Groups can be constituted so that it will help women to control the use of alcoholism in male members and spend money in the well being of the family.

Various technological innovations have been piloted in an attempt to eliminate wage payment delays and corruption. The Indian Institute of Technology (IIT) is currently developing a low-cost ATM machine that enables workers to easily obtain their wage payments, while Rajasthan is also working on a project to link biometric identification to banking with a smart-card. Another idea is for real-time MGNREGA transactions, using biometric data, smart phones, and/or GPS in addition to the use of voice-based or SMS technology to provide information when work is completed. In light of these and other efforts like these if used in Taungya communities,wage delays in MGNREGA can be overcome.

Implications of the Study

1. The livelihood strategies outlined in the study could be used as a basis for laying out a vocational training programme for Gujjar and Taungya with required skill set so that in the future, Livelihood is based on their indigenous knowledge and skill set identified through livelihood portfolios.
2. Literature base for the future researches.

Bibliography

Asha Sharma, 2012. SC/ST employment guarantee: women's empowerment in rural India by MGNREGA, *International Journal of Human Development and Management Sciences*, Vol. 1 No. 1, ISSN: 2250-8714.

Agyeman, V. K., 1998. *Impact of Social Forestry in Northern Ghana*. Report Submitted to Biodiversity Support Programme (BSP), USA, 30.

Agyeman, V. K., Kasanga, K. R., Danso, E., Marfo, K. A., Whiteman, A., Asare, A. B., Yeboah, O. M., and Agyeman, F., 2003. *Equitable Forest Reserve Plantation Revenue Sharing in Ghana.*

Awang, K., 1985. *Some Agroforestry Practices in Southeast Asia.* Occasional Paper No. 4. Faculty of Forestry, University Pertanian Malaysia, Serdang, Selangor.

Barna Maullick, 2009. Implication of NREGA District Barabanki, Uttar Pradesh, *Kurukshetra.*

Blanford, H. R.,1925. *Regeneration with the Assistance of Taungya in Burma.* Indian Forest records xi, Part III, 41.102.

Blanford, H. R.,1958. Highlights of one Hundred Years of Forestry in Burma. *Empire Forestry Review 27(1), 33-42.*

Brookman-Amissah, J., 1978. *Agroforestry Research in Ghana.* Paper Presented at Commonwealth Science Council Workshop, Malawi, June 1913.

Cincotta, R. and Pangare, G.,1993. Pastoralists: Brokers of Agricultural Soil fertility. *Wasteland News* VIII(3): 40-44.

Central Institute of Fisheries Education (CIFE), 2009. '*A Study Report on Appraisal on MGNREGA Programme in Thane and Akola Districts of Maharashtra'*, Report submitted to the Ministry of Rural Development/ UNDP, Mumbai, India.

Dheeraja, C., and H. Rao, 2010. *Changing Gender Relations: A Study of MGNREGS across Different States*', National Institute of Rural Development (NIRD), Hyderabad, India.

Dasgupta, S., and S. Sudarshan, 2011. '*Issues in Labour Market Inequality and Women's Participation in India's National Rural Employment Guarantee Act',* Working Paper No. 98, Geneva: International Labour Organisation.

Dreze, J., and R. Khera, 2011. *The Battle for Employment Guarantee,* ed. R. Khera, New Delhi: Oxford University Press, pp. 43–81.

Ellis, F. (2000). *Rural livelihoods and diversity in developing countries*. Oxford University Press.

Enabor, E. E., 1975. *Socio-economic Aspects of Taungya in Relation to Traditional Cultivation in Tropical Developing Countries*. FAO Soils Bull. No. 24, Food and Agriculture Organisation of the United Nations, Rome, 191-202.

Evans, J., 1982. *Plantation forestry in the tropics*. Oxford University Press, New York.

Evans, J., 1992. *Plantation forestry in the tropics: tree planting for industrial, social, environmental and agroforestry purpose* (2nd ed., 403). Oxford: Claredon Press.

Flintan, F., 2007a. "Sharing of Past Experiences" in *Gender and Pastoralism: Volume I: Rangeland and Resource Management in Ethiopia.* A. Ridgewell, G. Mamo and F. Flintan, Addis Ababa: SOS Sahel. Internet:http://www.sahel.org.uk/publications.html.

Gundeti Ramesh and T. Krishna Kumar, 2009.Facet of Rural Women Empowerment, *Kurukshetra*.

Gajaseni, J., 1990. *Socio-economic Aspects of Taungya in Taungya Forest Plantations with Agriculture in South-east Asia,* Redwood Press Ltd, Melkshan, UK.

Gorman, C. F., 1969. Haobinhian: Pebble-tool Complex with Early Plant Association in South East Asia, *Science* 163: 671-673.

Gosmami, P. C.,1982. Agroforestry Practices and Prospects as a Combined Land-use System, *Indian Forestry*. 108: 385.

Gregersen, H. M., 1982. *Environmental Constraints Versus Economic gain in Tropical forestry.*

Hazarika, P. G., 2009. *Promoting Women Empowerment and Gender Equality through the Right to Decent Work: Implementation of National Rural Employment Guarantee Program (NREGP) in Assam State (India)—A Case Study*, The Hague: Institute of Social Studies.

Hirway, I., and S. Batabyal, 2012. MGNREGA and Women's Empowerment,*UN Women South Asia*, New Delhi.

Hashemi, Syed M., Sidney Ruth Schuler and Ann P. Riley, 1996. Rural Credit Programs and Women's Empowerment in Bangladesh.*World Development* 24(4):635-653.

Hailey, L., 1957. *An African Survey,* Oxford University Press, Oxford, UK.

Huo, Y. Huo, 1992. Taungya in China, *Forest Plantations with Agriculture in Southeast Asia*, eds. C.F. Jordon, J. Gajaseni and H. Watanabe, 133- 146, Wallingford, U.K: CAB International.

Institute of Rural Management Anand (IRMA), 2010. *An Impact Assessment Study of the Usefulness and Sustainability of the Assets Created under Mahatma Gandhi Rural Employment Guarantee Act in Sikkim*, Anand: IRMA.

Jos Chathukulam, K. Gireesan, 2007. *Impact Assessment of NREGS in Kerala: Evaluation of systems and processes, Centre for Rural Management (CRM)*, Kottayam, Kerala, submitted to Ministry of Rural Development, Government of India, New Delhi.

Kartasubrata, J.,1997. *Tumpangsari method for establishment of teak plantations in Java; Proceedings of the symposium on Tropical Agricultural Technologies*,Tsukuha, Japan. Tropical Agricultural Research Report (Japan) 12, 141 – 152.

Kartasubrata, J.,1986. *Agroforestry in Indonesia with Special Reference to Tumpangsari in Forest Areas. Monsoon Asia Agroforestry Joint Research Team: Comparative Studies on Utilisation and Conservation of the Natural Environment by Agroforestry Systems*, 29-51, 107.

King, K. F. S., 1968. *Agri-silviculture (the Taungya System)*.Bulletin No.1 Ibadan University Press, Ibadan, Nigeria.

King, K. F. S.,1979. *Agroforestry: Proceedings of the Fiftieth Symposium on Tropical Agriculture.* Royal Tropical Institute, Amsterdam.

Khan, A. U., and M. R. Saluja, 2008. *Impact of the NREGP on Rural Livelihood*, Indian Development Foundation.

Khera, R., and N. Nayak, 2009. 'Women Workers and Perceptions of the National Rural Employment Guarantee Act', *Economic and Political Weekly*, Vol. 44, No. 43.

Khera, R., 2009. *'Group Measurement of NREGA Work: The Jalore Experiment'*, Delhi School of Economics,New Delhi.

Kumar Sambhav S. (2011). Taungyas get legal recognition. *Down to Earth.*

Ministry of Rural Development (MoRD), 2009-10. *Guidelines for Convergence: Leveraging NREGA for Sustainable Development through Inter-sectoral Convergence,* MoRD.

MacGillivray, A. W., 1990. Forest Use and Conflict in Burma, Imperial College of Science and Technology and Medicine, University of London. *Report Submitted in Partial Fulfilment of the Requirements for the MSc. Degree* and/or the DIC.108.

Narayan-Parker, D. (Ed.). (2005). *Measuring empowerment: cross-disciplinary perspectives*. World Bank Publications.

Narayan-Parker, D. (Ed.). (2002). *Empowerment and poverty reduction: A sourcebook*. World Bank Publications.

Nair, K. N., T. P. Sreedharan, and M. Anoopkumar, 2009. *A Study of National Rural Employment Guarantee Programme in Three Gram Panchayats of Kasargod District,* Thiruvananthapuram: Centre for Development Studies.

Nair, P. K. R. and Fernandes, E. C. M., 1984. *Agroforestry as an alternative to shifting cultivation. In: improved production system as an alternative to shifting cultivation.* FAO Soils Bulletin 53: 168-182. FAO Rome.

Nair, P. K. R., 1984. *Soil Productivity Aspects of Agroforestry*, ICRAF, Nairobi.

Nair, P. K. R., 1986. *Alternative and Improved Land Use Systems to Replace Resource-Depleting Shifting Cultivation. In: Strategies, Approaches and Systems for Integrated Watershed Management*. FAO Conservation Guide 14: 61-84. FAO, Rome.

Nair, P. K. R. (1989). *Agroforestry Systems in the Tropics*. Kluwer, Dordrecht.The Netherlands. 109.

Nayak, P. K., and Berkes, F. (2011). Commonisation and decommonisation: understanding the processes of change in the Chilika Lagoon, India. *Conservation and Society*, *9*(2), 132.

Pattanaik, B.K., 2007. NREGS – A micro appraisal of equity and efficiency, *IASSI Quarterly,* Vol. 26, 2007.

Pankaj, A. K., and A. N. Sharma,2008.*Understanding the Processes, Institutions and Mechanisms of Implementation and Impact Assessment of NREGA in Bihar and Jharkhand,* Institute of Human Development (IHD), New Delhi, India.

Pradhan, B., 2003. "Measuring Empowerment: A Methodological Approach" Development Vol. 46 Issue 2.*SID On-line Dialogue.*

Rigg, J. (2005). Poverty and livelihoods after fulltime farming: A South-east Asian view. *Asia Pacific Viewpoint*, *46*(2), 173-184.

Rituparna Bhattacharyya, Polly Vauquline, 2013. A Mirage or a Rural Life Line? Analysing the impact of Mahatma Gandhi Rural Employment Guarantee Act on Women Beneficiaries of Assam, *Space and Culture, India 2013, 1:1 http://www.spaceandculture.in/index.php/spaceandculture/article/view/10/1*

Poffenberger, Mark,1995. The Resurgence of Community forest Management in the Jungle Mahals of West Bengal, in David Arnold and Ram Chandra Guha(eds.). *Nature, Culture, Imperialism: Essays on the Environmental History of South Asia.* Delhi: Oxford University Press.

Ramakrishna, P.S., U.M. Chandrashekara, C. Elouard, C.Z. Guilmoto, R.K. Maikhuri, K.S. Rao, S. Sankar and K.G. Saxena (eds.), 2000. *Mountain Biodiversity, Land Use Dynamics and Traditional Ecological Knowledge.* Oxford & IBH, New Delhi, India.

Raghavan, M. S., 1960. *Genesis and History of the Kumri System of Cultivation. In*: Proceedings of the Nineth Silviculture Conference, Dehradun, 1956. Forest Research Institute, Dehradun, India.

Ruthenberg, H.,1980. *Farming Systems in the Tropics*. 2nd ed. Oxford University.

Segustrom, G.,1976. *Creating Work and caring about Workers in Tropical Countries*. Unasylva 114: 2-9.

Siregar, A. M., 1990. *Implementation of Agroforestry in Indonesia.In agroforestry Systems and Technologies,* BIOTROP Special Publication No. 39. South-east Asian Regional Centre for Tropical Biology. Bogor, Indonesia. 29-36.111.

Sumitro, A., 1990. *Agroforestry Development in Indonesia.*Paper Expert Consultation on agroforestry in the Asia-Pacific Region. FAO Regional Office for Asia and Pacific, Bangkok, Thailand.

Subhabrata Dutta, 2009. "NREGA in West Bengal: Success and Challenge", *Kurukshetra.*

Sourav Das, 2013. "Performance of Mahatma Gandhi National Rural Employment Guarantee Scheme with Special Reference to Hugli District of West Bengal", *The International Journal of Engineering And Science (IJES)*, Volume-2, Issue-5, Pages 01-05, 2013, ISSN (e): 2319-1813 ISSN (p): 2319-1805.

Srinivasa Rao Diddel, P. Muthaiyan, 2013. Employment Generation under MGNREGA in Tribals Andhra Pradesh Testimony of Five Years, *IOSR Journal of Humanities and Social Science (IOSR-JHSS)* Volume 9, Issue 4 (Mar. - Apr. 2013), pp. 55-64 e-ISSN: 2279-0837, p-ISSN: 2279-0845. www.Iosrjournals.Org.

SAMARTHAN, 2010. '*Impact Assessment of MGNREGA in Madhya Pradesh*', Submitted to Poverty Monitoring and Policy Support Unit (PMPSU), Madhya Pradesh: State Planning Commission.

Shah, T., S. Verma, R. Indu, and P. Hemant, 2010. *Asset Creation through Employment Guarantee?: Synthesis of Student Case Studies in Nine states of India*, International Water Management Institute (IWMI).

Sinha, R. K., and R. K. Marandi, 2011. *Impact of NREGA on Wage Rates Food Secuirty and Rural Urban Migration in Bihar,* Report submitted to the Ministry of Agriculture, Bhagalpur: Agro-economic Research Centre for Bihar and Jharkhand.

Sen, Gita. 1993. *Women's Empowerment and Human Rights: The Challenge to Policy.* Paper presented at the Population Summit of the World's Scientific Academies.

Tejwani, K. G., 1987. *Agroforestry Practices and Research in India*. In Gholz, H. L. (ed) Agroforestry: Realities, Possibilities and Potentials. Martinus Nijihoff, Dordrecht, 109-136.

Tripathi, A. (2011, May 20). Bonded labourers get land title after 70 years. *Times of India.*

Vaidya, C.V, 1924. *History of Medieval Hindu India*, Orient Book Supply Agency, Volume II, Poona, India.

Vaidya, C. S., and R. Singh, 2011. *Impact of NREGA on Wage Rate, Food Security and Rural Urban Migration in Himachal.*Shimla: Agro-economic Research Centre. Report submitted to the Ministry of Agriculture.

Vatta, K., D. K. Grover, and T. Grover, '*Impact of NREGA on Wage Rates, Food Security and Rural Urban Migration in Punjab*', Report submitted to Ministry of Agriculture, Ludhiana: Agro-Economic Research Center, Punjab Agriculture University, 2011.

Verma, S., 2011. *MGNREGA Assets and Rural Water Security: Synthesis of Field Studies in Bihar, Gujarat, Kerala and Rajasthan*, Anand: International Water Management Institute (IWMI).

Verma, S., 2012. *Labour Markets Dynamics in Post-MGNREGS Rural India,* Unpublished note shared with the Ministry of Rural Development.

Von Hesmer, H., 1966. *Der Kombiniete Land-und Forstwirschaftliche Anbau-I Tropisches Afrika.* Ernst Klett Verlag, Stuttgart, Germany.

Valdiya, K.S., 1987. *Environmental Geology: The Indian Context.* Tata Mcgraw Hill, New Delhi; 83pp.

Wanyeki, F. H. M., 1981. *Agroforestry Practices in High Potential Areas of Kenya.* In:Buck, L. (ed), Proceedings of the Kenya National Seminar on Agroforestry, 218-309. ICRAF, Nairobi.

Weaver, P. L.,1989. *Taungya Plantings in Puerto Rico Journal of Forestry* 87(3): 37-41.

White, K. J., 1985. *Intercrop Strategies and Practices in the Bhabar Terai of Central Nepal* (Manual No. 1) Ministry of Forests, Kathmandu, Nepal.

White, K. J., 1986. *Tree Farming Practices in the Bhabar Terai of Central Nepal* (Manual No. 2). Ministry of Forests Kathmandu, Nepal.

Wiersum, K. F. (ed), 1981. *Observations on Agroforestry on Java.* Forestry Faculty Gadjah Mada University, Yogyakarta, Indonesia & Department Forestry Management, Wageningen Agriculture University. Wageningen, the Neitherlands, 132.

Wiersum, K. F., 1982. *Tree Gardening and Taungya on Java: Examples of Agroforestry Techniques in the Humid Tropics.* Agroforestry Systems 1: 52-70.

Index

J

K

L

M

N

O

P